AF305062

Cromwell
Parliament's Crusading Politician

COGITO · ERGO · SUM
The Armorial Ensigns of
MICHAEL WOLFGANG LAURENCE
BARON NASEBY
One of Her Majesty's Most Honourable Privy Council
College of Arms
London
Garter Principal King of Arms

Cromwell

Parliament's Crusading Politician

MICHAEL NASEBY

THE RT. HON. THE LORD NASEBY PC

UNICORN

Published in 2026 by
Unicorn, an imprint of Unicorn Publishing Group
Charleston Studio
Meadow Business Centre
Lewes BN8 5RW
www.unicornpublishing.org

ISBN 978 1 917458 72 6
10 9 8 7 6 5 4 3 2 1

Design by newtonworks.uk
Printed in the UK by Bell & Bain Ltd, Glasgow

Contents

Dedication

This book is dedicated to my dear wife Ann who has supported my political career of more than sixty years since the very beginning. She has been my constant and cherished companion from the early years of tough initiation – from failing to win Islington North – a Labour stronghold – in 1966 to leading the Conservative campaign for Islington Council in 1968 and winning forty-seven of the sixty seats having held none before, and all the subsequent highs and inevitable lows that working in Westminster has brought us ever since.

Ann is a doctor. She trained at St Thomas's Hospital, Westminster before continuing her work at the SSKM Hospital in Calcutta, India where we lived while I worked for the Reckitt & Colman Group. On our return to the UK, she continued her work as a GP, setting up her own practice in Biggleswade, Bedfordshire, which she built up to a six-partner practice, only retiring in 1999. This she did, while raising our three children (and later, seven grandchildren) and supporting me throughout my career. Not only did she get actively involved with every election campaign but she also attended party conferences.

Throughout our sixty-five years of marriage, Ann and I have been lucky enough to travel the world and this has given us the unique and special opportunity to work together: each bringing our skill and knowledge from our respective professions. I can think of no better example than the aftermath of the Tsunami of Christmas 2004 which wreaked so much havoc and devastation in southeast Asia. Ann was by my side when, in early January 2005, we dropped everything to fly out to Sri Lanka to help in whatever ways we could: me as a politician, she as a doctor – dedicated to helping a country and its people that we both love so dearly in its hour of need.

I am in absolutely no doubt that my successful career in politics would never have been achieved but for my wonderful wife, Ann.

Acknowledgements

My grateful thanks to the following people for their time, expertise and professionalism in helping bring this book to fruition.

To archivists Nicholas Rogers and Duncan Rule at Sidney Sussex College, Cambridge; to Rev. Janet Wootton and her team at the Baptist Church, Bedford, including the team at the Bunyan Library; to Deputy Director of the Norris Museum in St Ives, Rachel Walmesley-Callagan; to David Beardmore for his knowledge on roads and conditions in Cromwell's time; to Simon Brown for information on non-conformity in Bedfordshire; to Sarah Bridges and Andy North of the Northamptonshire Archives Service; to Stuart Orme, Director of the Cromwell Museum, Huntingdon; to Louise Siddique of the Parliamentary Recording Unit; to Melissa Hamnett, Dr Katy Barrett and Penny McMahon at the Parliamentary Heritage and Archives; to the Lord Roberts of Belgravia; the Lord Magan of Castletown and the staff of the House of Lords' Library; to Lucie Skilton, my editor and the team at Unicorn.

Foreword

The Rt. Hon. Sir Lindsay Hoyle MP,
Speaker of the House of Commons

It is a great pleasure to write the Foreword for this book for Michael, Lord Naseby, who offers a fresh and unique perspective on one of British history's most complex figures: Oliver Cromwell.

Oliver Cromwell was Lord Protector of England, Scotland and Ireland from December 1653 until his death in September 1658. Prior to that he was a disciplined military leader and politician, fighting on battlefields the length and breadth of the country during the British Civil Wars as well as on political battlefields in Westminster as an elected MP, firstly for his hometown of Huntingdon and later for Cambridge. He oversaw the trial and execution of Charles I; his was the third signature on the death warrant which signalled the end of over 700 years of monarchical rule in England. Cromwell not only witnessed these extraordinary events but actively contributed to the formation of a new world order in the form of the Commonwealth of England. He was instrumental in the setting up of new procedures and protocols which heralded the arrival of a new way of governance.

With change there is inevitably resistance and with the Restoration of the Monarchy in 1660, history has often chosen to overlook the constitutional changes that were Cromwell's life work. Some of these changes, such as greater freedom in religion, we continue to enjoy in England today. Therefore, I am delighted that a long-standing parliamentary colleague Michael Naseby, still an active member of the House of Lords following twenty-three years serving in the House of Commons, wrote this new book which examines Oliver Cromwell in all his complexity: warrior, ruler, innovator and champion of parliamentary rule. It is this long experience at the heart of Westminster which enables him to assess Cromwell through the lens of one seasoned parliamentarian examining another.

This book offers a deeply personal reflection on the figure who has continued to inform and inspire Michael throughout his life in Westminster.

CHAPTER 1

'What's in a Name?': The Religious Landscape of Cromwell's World

I have been in Parliament since February 1974 when I was elected Member of Parliament for Northampton South on a majority of 179: the first Conservative MP for Northampton in fifty years. After twenty-three years of service, I lost my seat by 744 in the huge swing against John Major's government, at which time I was Chairman of Ways and Means and senior deputy to the Speaker of the House of Commons, Baroness Betty Boothroyd (sadly no longer with us). My last task on the floor of the House of Commons had been to chair the highly contentious Maastricht Bill (officially the Treaty on the European Union) to take the UK out of Europe. Consisting of four clauses, MPs proposed more than 500 amendments that were debated for twenty-five days, three of which continued all through the night, providing quite the challenge for my two deputies and me.

After the general election I was approached by both John Major, outgoing Conversative leader and Tony Blair, incoming Labour leader, asking if I was prepared to go to the House of Lords, to which my answer was a definite 'yes'. Once the appointment to the House of Lords had been formally announced the next part of the process was to sign in an acceptance and agree a title. In my case, 'Garter King', the person responsible, told me I could not be Lord Michael Morris, as there was already another Lord Michael Morris, and so I was asked to go away and think about a name that reflected my life. I thought about Northampton in all its dimensions. Then, Northampton's chief librarian asked if I was aware that most of the wounded from the Battle of Naseby – both parliamentarians and royalists – had been brought to three churches in Northampton, namely All Saints Church, St Giles and Holy Sepulchre. All three of them were in my constituency. I reflected: Naseby was the key battle in the First English Civil War resulting in our parliamentary democracy and now I knew that all those individuals who had suffered the most, from both sides, had been looked after in my constituency. This had real resonance. To me, the name Naseby felt synonymous with democracy and also reflected a tolerance, if not unity, between differing religious groups. I consulted the local council that covered Naseby village and they were more than pleased for me to use the name. And so, I became Lord Michael Naseby.

*

Despite all this, when I was at school and even at university, I was never very interested in politics. However, it was when I was working for Reckitt & Colman International in Sri Lanka, and a Sri Lankan friend was standing for Parliament there, that I got involved by using my professional experience by helping him with some publicity and marketing ideas. He got elected and rose to be Speaker of the Sri Lanka Parliament. His name was Ananda de Tissa de Alwis.

It was this experience that sowed the initial seeds and I became interested in politics in both the UK and Sri Lanka; an interest that developed and eventually came to underpin my life's work. In 2005, I was awarded the Presidential Honour of The Sri Lanka Ratna by President Chandrika Bandaranaike Kumaratunga; the highest award to foreigners. This was in recognition for the work I had done over the previous thirty years, from 1975 when I started the All Party UK Sri Lanka Group and supported the country through its huge challenges from 1975 until 2010.

Closer to home in the UK, in 2015, I was instrumental in getting a new Act on the statute book with a Private Members Bill; the Mutual Deferred Shares Act 2015, designed to facilitate capital-raising as well as equality of opportunity within the Mutual Movement. This not only took an enormous amount of energy, but also a comprehensive understanding of how our government and policy-making procedure works. For a Bill to go through Parliament it must be researched and drafted; put to the House of Commons – for which I needed to brief colleagues in the House as, by this time, I was in the Lords – to be debated and accepted before it could be passed as a law. The Parliamentary Archives team has informed me that this Bill is one of only four to receive royal assent in the previous decade. I feel particularly proud of this achievement as an important example of our parliamentary democracy in action as well as a testament to those of us, and I am one of many, who work hard to uphold it. It felt like a fitting culmination of my near half-century working in Westminster.

Reflecting back on where it all started, the years leading up to my being elected MP for Northampton South in 1974 gave me much valuable experience. In 1966, I stood for Parliament for Islington North, a rock-hard Labour seat which I did not win. However, due to the strength of my campaign and because I lived in Islington and knew, firsthand, the issues that were important to the local community, after the election, I was asked to lead the local Government campaign in Islington. The Conservative Party had no seats but, after a vigorous campaign which I led, we won forty-seven out of sixty seats. I was the first elected and, to date only, Conservative to be Leader of Islington Council. My lasting contribution was to save all the beautiful Georgian and Victorian squares which the Labour Council had started to demolish for council housing.

Throughout those twenty-three years I worked to gain experience at the very heart of politics in Westminster. For two years, I was the Parliamentary Private Secretary to the two Minsters of State in Northern Ireland, spending considerable time in Northern Ireland at the height of its troubles. I was appointed to the Public Accounts Committee – Parliament's investigatory committee for projects that have gone wrong; a role I held for over ten years. I was also appointed to the Council of Europe as one of the UK Government Members. A lasting memory was driving through the Health Committee's consolidation of autopsy procedures, across Europe, to be implemented after tragedies such as the sinking of the ship *The Herald of Free Enterprise* – the awful event which was the catalyst for the formation of the work.

In 1992, I was elected as senior deputy Speaker and Chairman of Ways and Means and it was in this role that, for the following five years, I chaired the annual debate on the Government's contentious budgets, faced with a packed chamber of excitable MP's. Add to this the extraordinary legislation following the country's vote for Brexit, I feel my experiences have helped me to understand in depth the challenges that Oliver Cromwell faced in his tenure as an MP and political leader. Both of us started out with an interest in politics at a local level; serving the communities in which we lived (which also happened to be the same geographical area of the Midlands); both of us worked in Westminster in roles that not only required commitment to and faith in the parliamentary system, however contentious the issue, but also demanded a deep understanding of the protocols and procedures to uphold that system. Both of us were posted to Ireland as part of our roles and responsibilities to a serving government. Both of us have experienced a country ravaged by civil war – Cromwell as a military leader in the English Civil War and me as a friend and former resident of Sri Lanka. The parallels are quite extraordinary and lend me, I feel, a truly unique and special perspective on Oliver Cromwell.

*

My own fascination with Cromwell began at a very early age and long before any formal study of the man. It started in Pinner, Middlesex, in 1943, where my parents, my younger brother and I had moved after returning from Bromyard in Herefordshire, where I had been evacuated during the Blitz.

My father had stayed in London as he was employed by the Ministry of Works, deployed every night after bombing by the Germans to sort out things on the ground. I was enrolled at St John's Prep School. In break times we used to have play battles between the Roundheads and the Cavaliers, and I was inevitably drawn to being a leader of the Roundheads. I also went to bible reading classes with a friend, which were held, if memory serves me correctly, at the Baptist Chapel. The group was called *Crusaders* and could perhaps be chalked up as my first contact with non-conformity. Incidentally, I looked up the definition of the word 'crusade' and in addition to the religious wars fought by Christians against the Muslims from the eleventh to the thirteenth centuries it is interesting to note that the *Oxford English Dictionary* states a crusade is 'a vigorous campaign for political, social or religious change' while the *Cambridge Dictionary* promotes 'a long and determined attempt to achieve, change or stop something because of strong beliefs'. I feel both are particularly relevant both to Oliver Cromwell and to me.

After St John's I went to Bedford School as a boarder. Bedford itself has a long history for being a hot bed of non-conformity with residents such as John Bunyan (1628–1688), author of *The Pilgrim's Progress from This World, to That Which Is to Come* (1678), among others. However, at the time, Bedford School was Church of England and the name Cromwell only really appeared in the syllabus for A level history. But I was fascinated.

*

Throughout his life, Oliver Cromwell was a dedicated Puritan – one of an estimated 20 per cent of the population of England and Wales in the seventeenth century. Puritans sought to 'purify' the Church of any remnants of Catholicism and aimed to live a humble and pure life, dedicated to God and not to His human representatives on Earth. Today, perhaps due to popular culture and important works such as Arthur Miller's play *The Crucible* (1953), the name 'Puritan' has connotations of severity, strictness and even joylessness. Ask any primary school-aged child about what it meant to be a Puritan and they will invariably answer, 'Puritans – and Oliver Cromwell – banned Christmas.' The truth of this claim is revealing: in 1647, the Puritan Government did indeed ban 25 December as a public holiday because there was no mention of the date in the Bible and they felt it was being used as an excuse for drunkenness, gambling and other forms of excess – and excess was the domain of the Catholics. Interestingly, however, Cromwell at this time was not part of the ruling government but away from London fighting in the provinces for other injustices, namely the under-payment of the military. So, history may have been unkind to our protagonist on this issue, painting him as a stern villain with the subtle complexities of his character lost over the passage of time. In fact, Cromwell believed that Liberty of conscience was a natural right: 'I meddle not with any man's conscience.' (Morrill, 2022), and that people should have the right to choose how they worshipped God – a democratic approach to worship that mirrored his belief in a democratic approach to secular governance.

In the sixteenth century, the vast majority of Protestants had simply been known as 'Puritan'. However, from the 1640s onwards, there was an increasing choice for individual families to choose to follow and worship, all grouped together under the heading of 'Dissenters and Non-conformists'. It is important to understand just how significant religious non-conformity was and to note that the groups that emerged during and after the Civil War didn't appear all at once. Some started in the late sixteenth century, others took shape amid the upheavals of the 1640s and 1650s and a few only became significant much later. However, setting them out in roughly chronological order helps show how one wave of religious change paved the way for the next.

Independents – also known as Congregationalists

The Independents had their beginnings in the late sixteenth century, when some reformminded members of the Elizabethan Church, frustrated by the lack of change from within, broke away to form their own congregations. This allowed them to choose and discipline their own ministers free from the authority of bishops. During the Civil War and the Interregnum, many independent churches were founded or expanded, with Cromwell's encouragement. In terms of belief, they didn't differ much from the Presbyterians; the real distinction lay in how each group thought the Church should be governed, but they still leaned heavily on Calvinist teaching – especially in their understanding of the Trinity.

Presbyterians

At the start of the Civil War, the Presbyterians were the dominant group on the parliamentary side. In 1646, Parliament even accepted the Westminster Assembly of Divines' recommendation that England should adopt a Presbyterian system of Church government. However, in practice, the plan never came to anything, and the national Church remained unreformed in that direction.

Baptists

Baptists took a very different view of baptism from the Church of England. They rejected the idea of baptising infants, arguing that the Bible showed baptism should come *after* someone had made their own, conscious declaration of faith. In other words, only those old enough to understand and publicly affirm their belief should be baptised. A few Baptist congregations existed in the early 1600s, but most sprang up during the 1650s, when religious experimentation was at its height. Even then, the movement wasn't entirely united. Particular Baptists followed Calvinist teaching and believed that salvation was reserved for the elect, chosen by God. General Baptists, by contrast, took a more Arminian view, holding that Christ's offer of salvation was open to everyone.

Quakers

The Society of Friends, or Quakers, originated in the 1650s and were part of the tolerance of differing faiths (albeit all

Protestant) under Cromwell's rule. At the heart of their faith was the belief that every individual could experience the 'Inner Light' of God directly, without the need for clergy or formal sacraments. The atmosphere of religious openness at the time allowed them to explore these ideas freely. Although they emerged during the Interregnum, they went on to prosper well into the eighteenth and nineteenth centuries, particularly in the North of England.

Unitarians

Unitarian ideas first took shape in the sixteenth century, particularly in Italy and Poland, before small groups began to appear in England and Wales. Although they were few in number during the Civil War period, the breakdown of old religious controls allowed more radical ideas to surface, including antiTrinitarian beliefs, which meant questioning the traditional Christian teaching that God exists as Father, Son and Holy Spirit. Figures such as John Biddle were already exploring these ideas in the 1640s and 1650s, laying the groundwork for what would later become organised Unitarianism. Even so, the movement developed only slowly, and its beliefs really came into their own in the late eighteenth century and early nineteenth.

Evangelicals

Evangelicals were not a denomination in their own right, and they only became a significant force in the eighteenth century. Even so, earlier movements and moments – stretching back to the late fifteenth century and early sixteenth – show clear 'evangelical' traits: a strong emphasis on personal conversion, Calvinist teaching and the use of openair preaching to reach ordinary people.

Methodism

Methodism began much later, in the 1730s, well outside the Civil War period. Its leading figure, John Wesley (1703–1791), was born long after the conflict and played no part in the events of the seventeenth century. Even so, Methodism became an important part of the wider story of English Dissent, drawing on many of the freedoms and traditions that had been born in the Civil War years. By the 1780s, there was even a distinct Calvinist Methodist branch.

The freedoms in religious thinking – and ways of worship – that had been allowed to flourish during the Civil War years came to an abrupt end after Cromwell's death and the restoration of the monarchy with the crowning of Charles II in 1660. The passing of the 1662 Act of Uniformity, and further acts in 1662 and 1664, sanctioned those who refused to conform to the Church of England's rules of worship. This blow resulted in some prominent Dissent leaders being imprisoned and, in effect, the penal legislation ensured that non-Anglican, non-card-carrying members of the established church became second-class citizens without basic political or social rights. Furthermore, it subjected some Baptists and Quakers to long periods of imprisonment and even transportation as slave labourers to the sugar and tobacco plantations of the Americas. Ironically, the Clarendon Code – introduced alongside the Act of Uniformity in 1662 – ended up creating a kind of religious divide in England. By excluding large numbers of Protestants from the Church of England, it actually strengthened the very groups it sought to suppress and helped give rise to a distinct tradition of English Protestant Nonconformity.

Two famous men stand out in this period of quasi-persecution:

John Milton (1608–1674), famous poet and also civil servant, wrote *A Treatise of Civil Power in Ecclesiastical Causes* and *Considerations Touching the Likeliest Means to Remove Hirelings out of the Church* (Milton, 1659) as a matched pair of pamphlets as well as the epic poem *Paradise Lost*, (Milton, 1674) the latter when he was blind and in a deep state of despair in reaction to the failure of the English Revolution. He had served as a civil servant for the Commonwealth under Oliver Cromwell. It was no coincidence that I chose to reference this poem (and its successor, *Paradise Regained*) in the subheading of my first book on Sri Lanka and its civil war.

John Bunyan (1628–1688), in his work *The Doctrine of Law and Grace Unfolded* (Bunyan, 1659), set out what has been called a 'politics of the will' – the idea that the elect could strengthen themselves spiritually in the face of persecution without turning to open rebellion. His own life soon tested that belief when, in 1661, he was imprisoned in the jail on Bedford Bridge – a place I later visited as a pupil at Bedford

School – and he remained there until 1672. It is hardly surprising that such long confinement gave him the time and inner focus to produce *The Pilgrim's Progress.*

Both these two strong-minded talented individuals were writing in a context where government has been radically destabilised and liberty of conscience was perceived to be under threat. I myself reflect when I was one of the UK Parliamentary Delegation on the Council of Europe in the 1990s listening with full attention to the speech from President Gorbachev about the future of a peaceful Europe only to witness, just thirty years later, the leader of the same country invade the sovereign independent nation of Ukraine.

So, what's in a name? A name does more than identify us; it connects us with those who share our beliefs and values. I feel very strongly that, despite living and working several centuries apart, I share many of the ideals and convictions that Cromwell strove to uphold. Yet, in the seventeenth century, naming your faith could not only define and unite you with fellow believers but could also cost you your liberty. It saddens me that this struggle continues today, as peoples and individuals alike fight for their identity to be recognised and respected. It is why I continue to promote the parliamentary cause – a system that upholds democratic rule through fair and representative governance and provides the arena in which even the most complex challenges can be discussed and debated and courses of action can be decided. When I entered the House of Lords, I had the privilege of choosing a name, and I chose one that reflected the values and convictions I hold dear, in honour of those who, hundreds of years before, fought for the right to bear their own, whether it was the name of their political affiliation or their faith.

CHAPTER 2

Cambridge – Twice Over

Oliver Cromwell's time at Sidney Sussex College, Cambridge is dismissed by many authors as a lost opportunity, as he neither completed his studies nor obtained a degree. In addition, it is alleged, he led a rather debauched life.

I had the privilege to go to Cambridge – to St Catharine's College – to read Economics after completing National Service in the Royal Air Force (RAF), culminating in my becoming a jet pilot. National Service took two years, which meant I was twenty rather eighteen when I started and, naturally, with no academic study in this period, I wondered what difficulties I would face.

It was a different story for Oliver Cromwell who went to Sidney Sussex College just two days short of his seventeenth birthday. Frankly by any yardstick he must have been excited, maybe relieved, not least leaving behind his family of sick father, mother and seven sisters younger than him. Did he really choose Sidney Sussex? I doubt it, as it seems far more likely that it was on the recommendation of the Montague family, close friends and neighbours of the family, not least as James Montague was the first Master.

Oliver was admitted on 23 April 1616 as a Fellow Commoner like other children from the gentry. This meant he would have the same food as College Fellows and it normally would have entitled him to a single room in Hall Court, the main building of the College. The only downside was that he would have to pay two shillings a quarter for necessary expenses. He was also required to present a piece of silver plate, sold soon after he left when the College had to repurchase land sold illegally. Sadly, the chapel Cromwell would have attended was demolished in 1776 but the communion plate he would have known still survives.

The College itself had only been founded in 1596. Its Statutes stated that the Master and Fellows were required to abhor 'Popery and all heresies, superstitions and errors' (*Statue Book for Sidney Sussex College, Cambridge*). This was no challenge to the first Master Samuel Ward who was a noted Calvinist theologian and one of the translators of the King James Bible. By 1616 Sidney Sussex was the sixth most popular college in Cambridge. This is not surprising because Calvinism within the Church of England was very popular.

What would Oliver study? In the early seventeenth century, the university curriculum was still based on the medieval scholastic system of the seven liberal arts. Like many of his contemporaries he did read for a degree, although, like many, he just studied the first part of the syllabus, known as the Trivium, covering grammar, rhetoric and logic. This was by no means an easy option but probably the most popular course and so Oliver and his twenty-one fellow students set forth.

Sheriff Smith of Glasgow possesses a notebook of George Palfrey, admitted later in the same year, which he kept during his undergraduate studies. This includes orations, sometimes touching on political matters, which students had to give both in College Hall and the University Schools, debating points and reading notes.

I myself have dug a little deeper and now have in my possession a copy of *The Rhetoric Syllabus*. Having read it carefully, the most revealing statement to me is: 'Rhetoric is likewise concerned with human passions and affections.' A leading contemporary academic Richard Holdsworth (1590–1649), Fellow of St John's and then Master of Emmanuel,

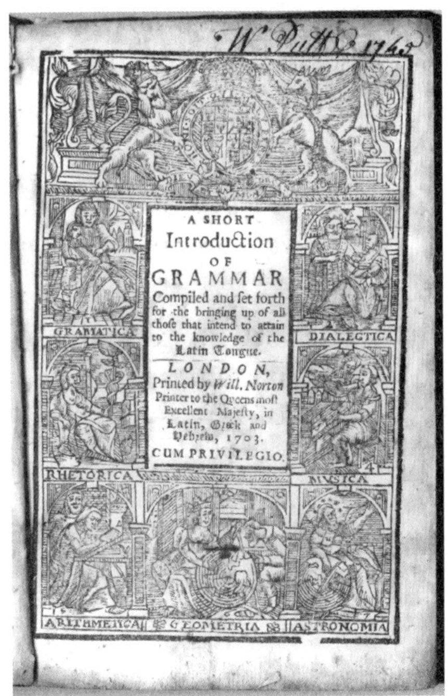

Rhetoric has been studied at the University of Cambridge since its inception in the Middle Ages, forming a core part of the arts curriculum for over 800 years. As part of the "trivium" (grammar, logic, and rhetoric), it was a foundation of early university study. (Wikimedia Commons).

until he was ejected in 1643, adapted a teaching practice that moved away from the traditional structure set out in the Elizabethan statutes, but certainly has resonance with me as a public speaker and politician.

> [Rhetoric]… teaches the nature of men's passions and affections, how to raise and move them, how to allay quiet and change them, a knowledge necessary not only in writing, but speeches and letters, but also in common discourse and dealing with men, if not to make use of it yourself at least to discover it to other men that you may not be at any time abused and overreached by it. (Holdsworth *c.* 1630)

Is it any wonder that Cromwell was such a good communicator when he had been taught these values? Whether in Parliament or in the military, providing inspired leadership was a vital necessity to his success. What a lesson to my fellow parliamentarians today who read from or continually refer to their laptop, removing any chance of colour or conviction in their speech. I wish when I was up someone would have taken the initiative to include 'Rhetoric' in our Economics syllabus. Furthermore, the very fact that Cromwell and his fellow students studied Rhetoric refutes the allegations that he wasted his time at Cambridge and his future career clearly demonstrates this view.

Of course there are the allegations of debauchery, playing football and loving the ale house, all of which were against College rules. Evidently, he did play football with a friend at

St John's College, and I don't doubt they went to an ale house: what student in any century has not been to the ale house or pub? However, there is no evidence that Cromwell did not take his work seriously. Most Fellow Commoners never intended to complete the degree as they and their parents viewed this university course as a form of finishing school giving them skills useful in public life.

The death of Cromwell's father on 24 June 1617 may well have precipitated his departure from the university and he did not return again until 1640, aged forty, when he was asked if he would stand as one of two MPs for Cambridge and was duly elected for the Short and Long Parliaments. Although there are no hard records regarding where he went after university, we know he did not return to Huntingdon straight away (except briefly to attend his father's funeral and attend to matters pertaining to his estate). It seems most likely that he went to London, probably to Lincoln's Inn to acquire a practical knowledge of law. Another fact that supports this idea is that three years later, on 22 August 1620, Oliver married Elizabeth Bourchier, daughter of a wealthy fur dealer, from London.

With a year of university education, three years of working in London and a new bride, Cromwell then returned to Huntingdon and moved in with his widowed mother and those sisters not yet married. They were not a rich family but there were family estates around Huntingdon needing to be properly managed, added to which his wife came with a comfortable endowment. Some would claim he took little interest in local affairs, but I find this hard to believe because in 1628 he was returned as one of two MPs for Huntingdon. Given what Cromwell went on to achieve, I believe he would have made good use of his time in Huntingdon, now settled both financially and domestically, to develop an interest in local politics. Living and working in a community, one cannot help but get involved: I have been in local politics myself. I agree there are some potential MPs steeped in the life of their hometown but there are others like me who helped a bit but had of necessity to focus on family and job to make ends meet. I imagine Cromwell did the same – in the process of working to provide for his family, he could not fail to take an interest in how his community was managed. Later in life, he proved to be a very shrewd businessman when, in 1657, he approved the Charter for the East India Company, ensuring England's monopoly of trade in the East. No doubt these early years in Huntingdon provided the training ground and gave him invaluable experience and skills in both business and politics.

Cromwell was aged just twenty-seven when, in March 1628, he was duly elected to be the Member of Parliament for Huntingdon. It is important to remember that at this time there were no political parties: Cromwell would have had a team of people on whom he could rely and ask for help, but essentially it was the person, the individual, who people voted for to represent them in Parliament. This is further evidence to support my idea that Cromwell did not let the grass grow under him while in Huntingdon in the 1620s.

There can be little doubt that MPs, veteran and new alike, must have known that Parliament was on shaky ground at this time. As any newly elected MP, Cromwell would have been briefed on the key issues that Parliament faced. In 1628, the most pressing concern was *The Petition of Right*, which was sowing the seeds of reducing the Crown's power, as it was concerned with 'laws against arbitrary arrests of citizens; laws against arbitrary imprisonment and laws defining the fundamental liberties of the Kingdom'. It had first been debated in the Commons in June 1625, re-introduced after the election of February 1626 and now, in 1628, was finally coming to fruition. The King, after years of vacillation, realised that if his monarchy was to survive, he would have to agree and so he did on 7 June 1628, just three months after the election of Cromwell. What a time for Cromwell to enter Parliament.

Cromwell would have been told he could not take part in the debate until he had made his maiden speech. I remember my first year as MP for Northampton South, winning on a majority of just 179. I had been a councillor in Islington, London but that was not much help in Northampton. I knew Harold Wilson only had a small majority and so I had to get my maiden speech in as early as possible while also attending regularly, voting as required and trying to understand procedure. So it was for Cromwell, too. He made his maiden speech on 11 February 1629 only for King Charles to dissolve Parliament a month later on 10 March 1629.

Records show that Cromwell's first speech was made in front of the House of Commons Grand Committee for Religion with John Pym MP in the chair. The subject was allegations against the bishop of Winchester, Richard Neile. Cromwell said: 'Dr Beard told him that one Dr Allabaster did att Spittle preach a sermon tenets of popery & Beard being to repeate the same, the now Bpp of Winton did send for Dr Bearde' (Cromwell, 1628).

Cromwell goes on to explain that Dr Beard was his headmaster at Huntingdon Grammar School. Some would claim it was bland, simply recounting reports of others practising 'popery', but in all my fifty years across both the House of Commons and the House of Lords those listening do not expect a revolutionary firebrand but usually a **résumé** of one's political and civilian life and maybe at the end some stimulating thought. So, actually, Cromwell's coming out to testify against a religious leader of high standing, in my opinion, was brave and showed not only the growing importance of his own faith but also that he had his finger on the political pulse.

Cromwell decided to give evidence to the Grand Committee for Religion primarily because it was a subject of growing importance to him, not least as he must have reflected on the strong Calvinist teaching at Cambridge, but he also knew the huge respect with which the chairman, Mr John Pym MP, was held. He must have found out or knew about a clergyman, the bishop of Lincoln, Richard Neile, who from 1614 to 1617 had allowed a clergyman under his jurisdiction, William Alabaster, to preach a sermon with Catholic overtones. For Cromwell the matter had been highlighted by his former headmaster, Thomas Beard. The House of Commons was already compiling a list of misdeeds by Bishop Neile, so Cromwell's evidence was well chosen.

The outcome as recorded was that Pym reported from the Committee to the House of Commons, which then ordered that the Speaker Sir John Finch should write to Beard instructing him to come to London to testify against Bishop Neile. Cromwell delivered the letter, but time was not on his side, as there were adjournments of the Committee and Parliament that prevented the Commons taking it any further.

Nevertheless, from Cromwell's point of view, it was a case of mission achieved: he had spoken out against a reported show of Catholicism, which not only showed the conviction of his own beliefs, but also demonstrated his understanding of the issues of the day. Even to this day, one of the favoured procedures with a difficult issue is to play for time, and Cromwell demonstrated his understanding of this tactic with this case. He must have thought that he had done a reasonable job in Westminster and would just have to wait for Parliament to be recalled but little did he know it would be another eleven years, and then only because the King was running out of money!

However, while Cromwell was away presenting his case against religious leaders in London, things were bubbling away in his hometown of Huntingdon. I suspect that there were some who felt that he was getting above his station or, at the very least, forgetting his constituents and their needs. This came to a head when a bequest to the town and discussions on how to spend it created animosity between the leading lights of the town and Cromwell. It came to the boil when Huntingdon's elite persuaded the Crown to create a new town charter that excluded, among others, the former MP Oliver Cromwell from being an alderman, and thus he would have no say in how the town was run. But they did not stop there, as, in the new charter, it was decreed that the mayor and aldermen were not just appointed for the year, but for life.

Cromwell was livid. Indeed, he was so outraged that he probably lost his temper publicly – not a clever thing to do with a royal charter. The issue hit the headlines – not just in Huntingdon but in London, too, resulting in Cromwell being hauled before the Privy Council. He was forced to make a humiliating public apology. Just as an aside, I have been on the Privy Council for twenty-eight years and nothing of this nature has come before us! Cromwell, being no fool, realised that his chances of being re-selected as MP for Huntingdon were now remote. This may seem parochial and provincial, but the effect was devastating for Cromwell and his family. I suspect that they felt ostracised by many and alienated from all that they knew. To be attacked in Parliament is one thing, but to be attacked by one's own community who one has sought to serve is quite another. Cromwell must have deliberated long and hard on what to do for the best for his family. The decision was made to sell up and move away from Huntingdon and have a fresh start in a new location. The family chose St Ives.

Cromwell and his family seemed to settle very quickly as he rented a pleasant home: a farmhouse behind Sleep Hall. It was just three minutes' walk to Church Gate. His old friend from Cambridge, Henry Downhall, had become a vicar in the town and would have been another good reason for the move there. Cromwell leased land and became a tenant farmer. In those days, St Ives was a thriving community complete with an important market. One has only to walk through the historic centre with its narrow streets today, as I have done, to enjoy its homely and welcoming feel. And on the drive from my home in Sandy, I sensed the true peace of the Fens and the traditional warmth and friendship found in this part of England.

Cromwell and family stayed in St Ives for nearly five years. This was a time for reflection and personal growth: no doubt there were long conversations with his friend, the local vicar, and, given how close it was, Cromwell must have visited Bedford, the home of other dissenting non-conformists, even if they were of other denominations. We know he came to the Baptist Chapel in Mill Street, and I also believe he must have heard of the young evangelical Bunyan, at the very least (even if it was before he penned *The Pilgrim's Progress*). So, for me, this settled, attractive and stimulating environment was perfect for Cromwell to be inspired to follow God's wishes as they came to him. Indeed, there is one piece of written evidence of his commitment to God. This is a letter to a Mr Storey in January 1636 concerning a lectureship at Godmanchester and reflects a feeling of quiet contentment in Cromwell's faith: 'The Lord hath by him wrought much good amongst us, "to him we lift up our hearts"' (Cromwell, 1636).

The element that is missing for me, therefore, is when and how did he become such an outspoken Puritan. I imagine that the tumultuous events that followed this peaceful time in St Ives would have hardened Cromwell and his beliefs. However, the seeds could have been sown by meeting with the young Lord of the Manor, Henry Lawrence, who was an extreme Puritan, coupled with his exposure to other non-conformists in Bedford. Our beliefs often settle into place when we find ourselves pushing back against the alternatives – the things we decide *not* to be can be just as formative as the things we embrace. Perhaps St Ives was Cromwell's fallow period. In agriculture, fallow land isn't idle; it's resting, restoring itself, quietly becoming capable of greater fertility. Perhaps those years were Cromwell's own fallow season, quietly preparing him for everything that followed.

At the beginning of 1636, Cromwell's financial fortunes changed as he inherited, from his maternal uncle, a series of long leases and administrations over property in and around Ely. He and his family moved again and quickly found a home near to St Mary's Church (which can be visited – as I have done). Comfortable now in his own religious beliefs as a Puritan, Cromwell joined the local group, which was part of a much larger organisation that probably covered Cambridge, St Ives, Huntingdon and even Bedford.

The whole of the English nation must have sensed trouble developing against Charles I's reign as the time with no Parliament called to sit stretched for longer and longer. Of course, there must have been those who were working away throughout those eleven long years with no Parliament, making sure they were ready to leap into action, but I doubt Cromwell was one of them. I imagine he was still cautious after having had his fingers burned in Huntingdon.

Thanks to the growing network of Puritans around the area, the Cambridge group may well have heard of Cromwell's impassioned stand against Fens drainage when he was in St Ives, which had given him significant exposure as both speaker and campaigner. As time moved on, and with his faith becoming more ardent, Cromwell must have begun to feel that any future request to serve in any form of leadership role, parliamentary or otherwise, would be God's calling.

Then, seemingly out of the blue, at the end of the Christmas holidays in 1639, a group of Puritans approached Cromwell to be one of the Members of Parliament for Cambridge–as and when an election was called. The very next day, he went to be sworn in as a freeman of Cambridge at the behest of the mayor.

Cromwell did not have long to wait as the election duly took place and he was returned as the Member of Parliament for Cambridge and Parliament was summonsed in April 1640.

The fallow period was over. Cromwell was ready.

CHAPTER 3

Cromwell, the Real Politician

'A week is a long time in politics.' The now immortal phrase first uttered by former Prime Minster Harold Wilson has perhaps never been truer than today. We are all subjected to news from every corner of the globe every waking moment of every day but even before technology being what it is today, a week has *always* been a long time in politics, as someone who has served for half a century I can testify. So, I cannot help but wonder how Cromwell really felt after a gap of eleven years from Parliament. It is an extraordinary length of time. Looking back eleven years from the time of writing, Queen Elizabeth II was in her seventh decade as reigning monarch, Barack Obama was President of the United States and David Cameron had just won an election and not yet raised the question of a referendum on the UK's place in Europe!

At the time of his election, Cromwell was forty-one and settled in an enjoyable and fruitful life in Ely – successful, respected and comfortably off. I was of a similar age – thirty-eight – when I won Northampton South, becoming the first Conservative MP for Northampton in fifty years. I remember feeling both excited and keen to get on with the job while also aware of the amount of work this would involve. I imagine Cromwell must have felt similar. Certainly, he was a new man compared to the one he was when, for a short time, he had been one of the two MPs for Huntingdon: a devoted Puritan who now had a mission in life and the drive to see it through thanks to his dedication to the Lord Spiritual, as well as the wisdom that his experiences of politics at local level had granted him. I feel sure he would have felt ready for the challenge, despite the length of time out.

The eleven years without Parliament were known as the Personal Rule – the autocratic rule of Charles I. During that time, Charles appointed Bishop William Laud as Archbishop of Canterbury, which many, including Puritans, felt was a move towards Catholicism. Allied to this was the fact that Charles's wife, Queen Henrietta Maria, was a fervent, practising Catholic with her own priest, masses and chapel at court. Across the country, weekly church attendance was compulsory, but many of the issues expounded in the sermons went against Puritan beliefs about how the holy day of Sunday should be spent. Cromwell spoke out from Ely and supported others who did so but, without a Parliament, frustrations could only bubble away and not be vented in any formal, public arena. To supress the religious dissenters, Charles responded with force: three Puritan writers who had printed a pamphlet, *News from Ipswich*, were put on trial, found guilty and received severe punishment. The main author, William Prynne, was not only fined but pilloried and had his ears cropped. This was not an isolated case and sent a very clear message from the Crown: religious dissent would not be tolerated.

Added to the growing religious tension was the general economic state of the nation, which in 1630 – and again later in 1640 – had suffered from poor harvest, causing considerable poverty among the people. During this time, Cromwell, as local Cambridgeshire resident with a social conscience underpinned by his faith, had taken up the cause of the drainage of the Fens. His particular challenge was the 'Great Level'. This was led by the Duke of Bedford who was spokesman for the landowners. The concept was clear: marshland that was normally flooded would be brought back into use by draining a particular Fen so that small and large farmers alike could grow crops on the land and even have pasture for cattle, safe in the knowledge that the land would not be flooded again. The principle was clear enough and the know-how was certainly there. The challenge was how to get a fair deal for all the parties involved; while drainage had practical advantages it also threatened the traditional common rights of smallholders, which could leave them without a viable living. Cromwell, motivated by his own deep sense of social consciousness, took the side of the local inhabitants and negotiated on their behalf with the Duke of Bedford. Together they created a sort of code of how to share the land reasonably and equitably. Later, this earned Cromwell the title of 'Lord of the Fens'. It was awarded to him by his enemies, no doubt intended to belittle him and remind him of his work at a parochial level, but I like to think he would have been proud of his service to his fellow citizen at a small and local level.

At a national level the King was facing financial challenges but still refused to recall Parliament. Historically, there had been a levy on coastal towns during times of emergency to bolster their defences. Charles decided to make this into a national tax, named 'ship money', and, without a Parliament, there could be no public debate, let alone resistance. Cromwell's cousin John Hampden refused to pay ship money, resulting in a trial being brought against him. He lost on the grounds that 'The King is the law' and found himself sent to prison. The King's lawyers stated it was for the King alone to decide if there was a national danger requiring extra taxation. One can just imagine the reaction in the wider Cromwell family let alone the whole of the Puritan fraternity who already felt they were being discriminated against.

Troubles kept rumbling for the King but were not just limited to England: the Scots had also opened up their own front of protest, not surprisingly about religion and taxation. It is said that Charles I never liked Scotland nor understood the Scots. Perhaps because they were noted for their care where money was concerned, quite the opposite of Charles and his entourage, and therefore had not taken kindly to the new heavy taxation that had seen a near-trebling of the amount due from approximately £50,000 to £150,000. To cap it all, in 1637 a new liturgy for Scotland was published, which demanded Royal prerogative. The Scots responded with their own National Covenant, drafted by Scottish lawyers, with a reminder to the King of his solemn oath and the supremacy of Parliament. Charles's counter-attack was to insist on conformity, by force, and this led to the First Bishop's War in 1639. Cromwell was not directly involved or affected by what was happening north of the border but by a strange twist of fate he housed some of the commanders of the English army at his home in Ely and to whom he stated his strong objection to the King's actions. I feel certain that word must have got back to the King about this man: Oliver Cromwell, Puritan and representative of the ordinary people.

Inevitably, the King found himself facing a shortage of revenue to pay for the Scots war and realised he needed Parliament to raise it. So, in April 1640 elections were held. Cromwell had been approached to stand for Cambridge along with Thomas Meautys, Clerk of the Privy Council, a government nominee. By now, Cromwell was well-known with good family connections and had a proven track record thanks to his work on the Fens drainage project. In addition, even in his limited time in Parliament as MP for Huntingdon, he had built a relationship with John Pym (not related to the Bedfordshire Pym's). He was duly elected as MP for Cambridge and it was thanks to Pym that Cromwell soon found lodgings in Long Acre near Covent Garden, London. He was ready to attend Parliament.

*

The majority of the MPs returned to Parliament in April 1640 had served in the previous Parliament back in 1629 and, as previously stated, we can only imagine how extraordinary it must have felt after such a long absence. If eleven years was a long time then the few short weeks that followed, in what became known as the Short Parliament, were equally extraordinary – long enough for John Pym to deliver a two-hour oration calling for a new consideration of the rights of Parliament. Delivered with conviction, he called for a general redress of grievances, both political and religious, by the King. He ended by asking for annual Parliaments; pointing out that the long intermittent sessions were contrary to the two statutes still in force. How I would have loved to have been with Cromwell, sitting on the back benches hanging on every word, listening to Pym's exposition, rising to a climax. Then, with colleagues all around, as if with one voice, sending up a cry of 'Good Oration!'

Did Cromwell himself say anything in the time of the Short Parliament? We know from comments of others that he attended but there are no records of speech or contributions from him. One might dismiss this as his being a bit rusty or perhaps lacking in confidence, having not been in Westminster for so long. However, I do not find this surprising because of the feverish atmosphere created by the tension between senior experienced parliamentarians and the uncooperative attitude of the King. I prefer to think of him as the shrewd observer in this volatile arena, waiting, biding his time.

I suspect that Cromwell may well have decided to find out how the whole of the parliamentary system really worked, rather than just observing fiery debate in the House of Commons. If he did, he must have realised just how different the two Houses were and how much there was to learn. Since 1621, the House of Lords had operated within a set of Standing Orders with thirty-three itemised clauses amounting to about 2,000 words. In stark contrast, there was nothing written down about the protocols and procedures for the House of Commons. As he dug a little deeper, he would have found that information covered by the Standing Orders included a dizzying array of topics from the role of 'The Lord Speaker' to members' seating arrangements, as well as voting, fines for members late to the House, and specification of the number of members permitted to speak during a debate. Then, in 1624 new clauses were added, and again in 1626 matters move further forward with the addition of the procedure for the Clerk to read out the Standing Orders ahead of anything else. And yet, there was still nothing written down about conduct or procedure for the House of Commons. Given this contrast, I imagine Cromwell must have understood why he knew so little of the workings of Parliament from his year in office as MP for Huntingdon between March 1628 and March 1629.

Records show that, once he had got to grips with how the two Houses worked, Cromwell was really active in Parliament from 1641 onwards. I imagine he must have felt relieved that the House of Commons was not so constrained by written rules and protocols and allowed him to press ahead with matters of importance.

In actuality, after Pym's rousing speech, allied to continuing problems in Scotland, the King and his advisors decided to dissolve Parliament and prepare their ground for the future. However, the pressing need for finance left them no choice but to recall Parliament later that same year, on 3 November. Cromwell was duly elected again but his compatriot was new

– John Lowry a local Puritan man who defeated Thomas Meautys at the selection process in Cambridge. I can certainly sympathise as I had a similar experience of being 'a new boy' in Parliament when I was first elected as an MP in February 1974 only to have to face another election in October of the same year, too.

Having got a taste of what parliamentary life was like, hearing impassioned speeches in the House of Commons and then ready to join the debate, Cromwell must have felt enormous frustration when Parliament was dissolved. But I like to think that this only fuelled his fire and ambition, which continued to grow throughout the short recess. I am confident he was determined to play a key role in establishing the proper rights of Parliament, which would govern over and above any Divine Right of Kings, and the evidence supports this. When Parliament is returned, he loses no time by speaking on 30 December about the need for annual Parliaments, regardless of whether the King sends out his writ or not: 'the Bill touching the holding of a Parliament everie yeare, whether the king sends out his writt or not wch Mr Stroud preferred might bee read the second time' (Cromwell, 1640).

Cromwell was supported and the Bill went to Committee – of which he was a member. After much debate the length of time was extended to three years but eventually passed into law as the 1641 Triennial Act. It may have been longer than Cromwell would have wanted but it was a seismic shift away from the autocratic rule of a monarch and therefore an important win for Cromwell and his fellow parliamentarians.

In 1641, he is hot out of the blocks making no less than fifty-three speeches followed by another fifty-four in 1642. This is no mean achievement and would be impossible today, but what it does demonstrate, very clearly, is Cromwell's commitment as a true, active parliamentarian, which he had never been before.

I have read all these speeches, which have certain common threads. He speaks regularly on matters affecting his constituency of Cambridge and the surrounding areas of Eastern England. He appears to be careful to speak only on key areas of which he has knowledge or that he sees as fundamental to the success of the country. In addition to these formal speeches in the House, MPs would also be expected to debate important issues in committee and Cromwell was certainly active here, too. It remains as true today as much as it did in Cromwell's time that if you, a parliamentarian, want to be noticed, taken seriously or want to achieve change then you must take part in debates, speak with clear conviction and be prepared to follow up with oral questions and motions for debate.

Religion was always a hot topic about which Cromwell was particularly passionate. At this time, the question of uniformity in faith continued to be discussed: key for the Presbyterians but rejected by Independents, of which Cromwell was a leading figure. There is evidence of his being summoned to the bar of the House of Commons to apologise for using unacceptable language, which makes me smile. Oliver, the devout Puritan, the previously cautious yet observant politician and the defender of the rights of the common man being so moved by his own convictions that he resorts to bad language. Proof that he was human after all!

In 1641 he made twenty-five major speeches in the House of Commons. The breakdown of the subject of these is:

Religion: 8
Parliamentary procedure: 8
Cambridge: 4
Military matters: 5

In 1642, his incredible work ethic is clearly evident with records of a staggering fifty-six speeches made. But this time, the subject matter is markedly different:

Parliamentary matters: 22
Defence: 20
Irish: 14

Reading the list of topics discussed clearly demonstrates two things to me. The first is that Parliament is now finding its feet; it has established its procedures and is seen to be working democratically and somewhat openly; regularly discussing 'Parliamentary matters'. This is a world away from the King's Personal Rule. Secondly, there is a shift in focus from localised, domestic issues to international concerns. 'Defence' taking up so much time and resource signals unease and unrest and Parliament's concern that war is coming.

The Irish Questions arose out of the Irish rising of October 1641, which saw clashes between Irish Catholic landowners and newer, Protestant English settlers but with far-reaching consequences for England and Charles I's rule. No doubt Ireland felt a long way away to Cromwell at this time, but stories of Catholics wreaking havoc on Protestants, no doubt embellished for dramatic effect in their re-telling as they travelled over the seas, would have touched a nerve. The Rising also created a constitutional crisis. Parliament feared that if England's military command was given to Charles, intended to suppress the Irish uprising, the King may then use the same military force against his English opponents if things didn't go his way.

In some ways the ghastly news of increased violence against Protestants in Ireland created an impetus and catalyst to bring forward the Grand Remonstrance. Essentially, this was a wide-ranging attack on the position of the monarchy, which was to be debated on 1 November. There was widespread concern that control of the military should not belong to the Crown – a view that Cromwell would have totally supported. The wind-up debate on the Grand Remonstrance took place on 22 November. Strangely, Cromwell did not take part, but his view on this important subject was recorded in an aside to Falkland: 'If the Remonstrance had been rejected he would have sold all he had the next morning, and never have seen England more; and he knew there were many other honest men of the same resolution' (Cromwell, 1636).

In the King's eyes, Parliament was not just 'anti-Royal' but a blatant opposition to his 'Divine Right' to be King. His authority was under attack and no doubt his patience had been sorely tested, too. More than this, he must have felt he was losing the respect of his MPs and, on 4 January 1642, in a moment of hot-heated vanity, he stormed into Parliament. His intention had been to demand the arrest of five members who he believed to be ringleaders in the rising opposition to his rule: John Pym, John Hampden, Sir Arthur Hazelrig, Denzil Holles and William Strode. However, the King had made the mistake of instructing the Attorney General to impeach the five Members for Treason, allowing the intended culprits to be given a head's up. In a flurry, the King rushes down to Parliament accompanied by his bodyguards demanding the arrest of the five, only to find that the birds have flown downstream to the City and were nowhere to be seen. He bursts through the door, plops into his chair and demands of Speaker Lenthall to know the whereabouts of the missing Members. The notorious response was: 'May it pleasure your Majesty, I have neither eyes to see nor tongue to speak in this place but as the House is pleased to direct me whose servant I am here' (Speaker Lenthall, 1642).

Once again, I wish I had been able to sit next to Cromwell on the right-hand side of the chair, the side of government, to hear this. I am sure Cromwell would not have been silent.

The result was that the King had had enough of Parliament and decided to leave London, never to return until his death. However, it would be another eight months before he raised his standard at Nottingham to signal the start of the first battle of the Civil War.

In these months, two significant events took place. First, on a procedural level, was the listing of Nineteen Propositions for the King to sign – a sort of wish-list from Parliament to reduce the power of the monarch. I say 'wish-list' because there was never any chance that the King would agree to any of them, let alone all of them. The propositions included demands such as the King's children may not marry anyone without the consent of Parliament and the King must accept the ordering of the military by the House of Commons and House of Lords.

The second event, or activity, were the preparations for war – more probable than possible by this point. Cromwell did his bit to double check on the Tower of London, the Lord Mayor of London and the City Fathers, ensuring they were all on side, the parliamentary side, and then set off at speed for Cambridge.

The country was in turmoil: up and down the country, the King's Commissioners were trying to raise troops for the King and, at the same time, raise funds. In Cambridge, Cromwell rushed to prevent silver, plate and funds from the colleges going to the King: a timely and successful operation. The amount saved by Cromwell was reported to Parliament to be worth £20,000. The figure of £20,000 would be an enormous sum today, likely exceeding £4 to £5 million. This really does show that if an MP is close to and looks after his constituency, wonders can be achieved.

Wars, to be fought successfully, need strong leadership. We only need to look back across history to see this: Winston

Churchill will be remembered as one of the great British leaders of all time, thanks to his leadership through the Second World War. At the onset of the Civil War, Cromwell, the parliamentarian, the devout Puritan, looking back over the previous decade of increasing unhappiness with the way his country was being ruled, reflected: 'Religion was not the thing at first contested for; but God brought it to that issue at last: and it proved that which was most dear to us'. (Cromwell, 1655).

Milton, arguably my favourite poet, captures beautifully how Cromwell's journey of faith, coupled with his experiences as a politician, provided him with the necessary skills needed in conflict. Skills that, by the spring of 1642, would not only be valued but would be vital for the tumultuous months ahead. 'He first acquired the government of himself, and over himself acquired the most signal victories so that on the first day he took the field against the external enemy, he was a veteran in arms, consummately practised in the toils and exigencies of war' (Milton, 1654).

CHAPTER 4

Civil War

Cromwell was named as one of eighty men who were awarded the rank of captain and tasked with raising troops. Each was given a budget by Parliament of up to £1,104 to do this. At this time, there was no such thing as a standing army; in fact the only troops at all were the Royal Bodyguards and the 'Trained Bands' and they were only in London. The basic task of raising an army for Parliament rested with the County Lord Lieutenants supported by their local MPs.

Cromwell knows what to do and, starting in Huntingdon in the late summer of 1642, quickly raises a troop of sixty horsemen. He could scarcely have imagined that, from the autumn of 1642 to the summer of 1646, his life would be utterly consumed by war. Yet, as politicians during both the First and Second World Wars – not to mention countless others – would discover, conflicts have a habit of lasting far longer than anyone anticipates.

I reflected on Cromwell: here he was, a full-time politician, aged forty-three, who yes could ride a horse well following his years as a member of the local gentry and work as tenant farmer, and it is possible that he knew how to use both a sword and a musket, but in terms of his experiences of the realities of war, he had none. Here am I, aged eighty-nine, reflecting on my own experiences of war, conflict and military training. At the age of four, I was evacuated to Bromyard, Herefordshire, together with my mother and younger brother, because of the Blitz in London. My father was left behind, working for the Ministry of Works, to ensure that every morning after the previous night's assault, London and her citizens got back up and carried on with true British grit and determination. Later, at age eighteen, I was enrolled for two years compulsory National Service in the RAF. I was posted to Canada to participate in a nine-month training programme to learn how to fly piston-engined Harvards and then spent a further five months flying T-33 fast jets. This was part of a North Atlantic Treaty Organization (NATO) initiative where Canada offered to host and train pilots from ten other NATO countries. It was an incredible experience (documented in my book *The Few Who Flew*, Unicorn, 2022), and one I shall always cherish: all those who completed the course earned their Wings, and mine still reside in pride of place at my home.

This amounts to considerably more experience than Oliver Cromwell had had by the time he was called upon to be a fighting captain. No longer a young man, he was rushing around on horseback seeking support for the parliamentary cause be it in kind or cash, but all aimed to promote Parliament's cause against the King. At the same time, he was overseeing the defences of Cambridge. However, this was not a short campaign, but one that continued for years. In fact, these years at the front-line of the Civil War were to shape him and, in a speech of 1657, he reflected that his military experiences had cemented his political and religious aspirations, too.

In practical terms, his priority was to raise money to look after his men – and their horses. Cromwell, by now, was well-versed in managing operations and logistics, from his work as a land agent, tenant farmer and MP. Where his experience of the battlefield was lacking, it was more than made up in his ability to organise and administrate. He ensured that the soldiers who served under him were not only properly armed but that their religious and moral welfare was catered for too: troops were issued with a copy of *The Soldier's Pocket Bible*. Launched in 1643, Cromwell oversaw its production and ensured every soldier had a copy. All evidence suggests he was very successful. I do not think this is surprising as he was well known in Eastern England and given the serious nature of the task to help Parliament, people responded.

I had a similar experience when asked to raise money for *The Victoria County History Project on Northamptonshire*. The mission of the group was to bring together volunteers, contractors and others to research and write a history of the town of Towcester and its surrounding villages. I raised several thousand pounds because people recognised not only the importance of the subject, but also its relevance to them and were prepared to trust me as their local MP.

All of the hard work – promoting the cause, planning for war and preparing soldiers – finally came to be used when, on

23 October 1642, a summons came for Captain Cromwell to meet the Earl of Essex and take part in the Battle of Edgehill. It appears that he arrived too late to play a significant role, but he did help near the end. It is alleged he followed Essex to Turnham Green just to the West of London to stop the King entering London, but I have my doubts. Needless to say, much like his first experience of Parliament, his first experience of war, even if as an observant bystander, gave him invaluable experience for what was to come, not to mention his innate sense of timing, both on and off the battlefield.

Back in Eastern England he was soon fighting a series of skirmishes at Lowestoft, bombarding Crowland Abbey and Burghley House. Cromwell then experienced more sustained field actions, at Belton in May 1643 and at Gainsborough in July, before winning the Battle of Winceby in October. In December he was, not surprisingly, promoted to lieutenant general. Between these times, he had ensured that the defences of Cambridge, Huntingdon, Peterborough and Ely were secure. Technically, his units were a part of the Eastern Association.

I believe that, despite his age and lack of previous experience, there were a number of factors that combined to ensure Cromwell's battlefield success. He was evidently a quick learner and a responsive one, too. Being an accomplished horseman meant that he was a good fit in the Cavalry and understood its powerful potential: he soon recognised that one cavalry troop was the equivalent to three troops of foot soldiers. He developed new tactics like the cavalry charge and learned not to gallop away after a successful charge. His ability to learn through observation, from his time in the House of Commons when there were no written rules, furnished him with the ability to read a situation, quickly, and adapt to it. Coupled with this was his self-discipline and his unshakable faith, which meant he led by powerful example: he looked after the well-being of his men – fundraising locally for their equipment – and reminding his junior officers that they must be honest, sober, godly and disciplined.

Following his promotion Cromwell became second in command of the army of the Eastern Association under the Earl of Manchester. The year 1644 was one dominated by war: his units took part in the key battles of Marston Moor on 2 July and Newbury on 27 October, excelling in both and thus further promoting their cause to overthrow the monarchy.

What I find amazing is that during this tumultuous time of fighting on a battlefield, he still managed to keep in touch with Parliament, which was sitting through the whole course of the first Civil War. In 1642, he had made two speeches, both on 16 July. One was about the impeachment of the Lord Mayor of London and the other on Irish Affairs. This was less than two months before he was on the battlefield at Edghill. In 1643, despite being heavily involved in the bloody business of warfare, incredibly, he manages to write no less than thirty-five letters to various key people in Parliament. In 1644, he finds time to return to London to make two important speeches. The first, on 22 January, criticising the leadership of Lord Willoughby of Parham. The second, on 25 November (my birthday), criticising the Earl of Manchester and suggesting he be removed from office. The diary of Sir Simonds D'Ewes reads:

> I went back into the House a little before 11 o'clock. I found Oliver Cromwell speaking vehemently against Edward Montague, Earl of Manchester as though he was on trial because the armies of Parliament had achieved nothing at Newbury and Aldermaston. Cromwell himself highlighted the fact that all his men were very desirous to fight not least the Independents. (D'Ewes, 1644)

The outcome was that Cromwell's speech was delivered with 'soe much cleareness and ingenuitie yt the howses Rested sattisfied yr with' (D'Ewes, 1644). It was then referred to the Commons to its Committee on the Lord General's army, chaired by Zouch Tate MP for Northampton. (Good to see a former MP for my constituency playing such a senior role!)

Once again, he sends thirty-three official letters to Parliament, which I have read. At the heart of this activity, I believe, was Cromwell's belief that Parliament needed to offer strong leadership, with a clear strategy that established who held overall command of the army and what it was meant to achieve in the field.

As an MP, Cromwell would have known the Earl of Essex, Robert Devereux, Parliament's Lord General, and I believe he respected him, a little. However, Essex was not a free agent because his commission stated he was to obey the direction of both the Houses of Parliament. This was to be implemented by an advisory committee of all peers and MPs serving in the army. The only safeguard was that they could only raise issues initiated by Essex. The objective was to ensure that orders from Westminster were understood and acted upon.

Essex's remit was to do all he could to bring the King to his senses and to prevent the monarch's supporters from raising troops in South and Central England. He certainly achieved the first objective and prevented the King advancing on London, but his successes in restricting the royalist build up elsewhere were minimal. It seems he was a bit prickly with a propensity to take offence (which seems to have boiled over into his relationship with Sir William Waller during the campaign in the South of England during 1643 and 1644).

A further example of the precariousness of Essex's position is recorded in his departure from London to join his army headquarters in Northampton, my former constituency. It is reported that he set off through crowds of ordinary people and up to Highgate Hill, which was lined with the 'city trained bands' almost certainly sent by the Lord Mayor. As he left Parliament, a certain Lord Robartes addressed him on behalf of the two Houses: 'the tongues of the Commons united together so with utmost strength of goodwill cry out "vivat" Roy and Essex, God save the King and the general good of the kingdom' (D'Ewes, 1644).

I took the same route to my constituency in Northampton thousands of times, but with no supporters in sight and certainly never a send-off like this. This leads me to presume that Essex needed that public support, even if staged, and that paradoxically belies a fragile ego. It is a well-known political strategy to bolster weaker members of a party by lending them the support of a stronger counterpart.

There are plenty of history books that record the to-ing and fro-ing of the battlefield. However, I am more concerned with the impact that these political skirmishes had on Cromwell and his small army and the relationship between the two: government and military. Minute books were kept to record what was happening out in the battlefield, but I wonder how much of that brutal and bloody reality could be understood by those who stayed in London and did not participate in the fighting themselves?

So it seems that the movers and shakers in Parliament were not particularly happy with Essex but there was no obvious successor. Instead, the idea of setting up an alternative army was floated. However, the concept could not really work for similar reasons: who had both military and parliamentary experience? Candidates came and went, such as Sir William Waller, Lord Grey of Wark and Lord Manchester. Waller became the most likely candidate, but his recruiting ability began to be questioned and there was also the problem of his failed leadership at Newbury.

Given the dilemma of finding someone suitable to set up a new army, one might wonder why Parliament was not more active in promoting action against the King. The truth seems to be that John Pym was able, with all his experience, to manage Parliament and he supported Essex. Together they kept a reasonably successful partnership between military and government or, at least, maintained the delicate status quo. However, Pym died in December 1643, which finally allowed two of the different factions in the Commons to go head-to-head: either end the war by negotiating with the King or end negotiation and go for outright military victory.

Politically, matters were already stirring. An ordinance established the Committee of Both Kingdoms (England and Scotland) that was to determine strategy, oversee military operations and allocate military resources. It was introduced by Essex on 1 February 1644 and then returned by the Lords with amendments. This now read: 'to advise, consult, order and direct concerning the managing of the war'.

After just a few days of reflection, the Lord General Essex proposed the third reading of the ordinance and it came into effect; the consequences of it finally broke the stalemate and facilitated the start of a way forward.

On 8 May 1644, the Committee of Both Kingdoms ordered Essex and Waller to seek out the King's forces wherever they were in the South and South-West. Initially, they made good progress despite there being no real triumphs. Then the temptation faced them to relieve Plymouth, which was achieved. Full of confidence they moved forward to Cornwall only to meet the royalist army, head-on, who surrounded them in a narrow peninsula between Lostwithiel and Fowey. The parliamentarians were forced to surrender, although Essex managed to escape in a fishing boat.

The disaster at Lostwithiel was soon seen as an opportunity to further progress the concept of the New Model Army and in early October 1644 Parliament passed an ordinance to combine Essex's, Waller's and Manchester's forces into a single entity under the direct control of a sub-committee of the Committee of Both Kingdoms.

On 19 November 1644, the House of Commons ordered the Committee of Both Kingdoms 'to consider the state and condition of all the forces under the command of Parliament and to put them in such a posture as may make them useful and advantageous to the kingdom'.

One might think those responsible would have acted speedily but they did not presumably because from 17 to 21 November, the Committee of Both Kingdoms had received no intelligence at all from the army group. Not surprisingly MPs wanted action. They expanded their previous resolution so that it focused on remodelling and tore up previous ordinances of the armies of Essex, Manchester and Waller. I suspect both Cromwell and Waller got wind of what was going on so they hurried back to Westminster, arriving two days before the second resolution was passed.

The Commons demanded an explanation regarding what had happened when the two armies met up on 20 October. Cromwell appears to have put the blame squarely with Lord

Essex. However, at the back of his mind, he realised Essex's days were ending and his real enemy was Earl Manchester. Emboldened by his experiences on the battlefield, resolute in his faith, Cromwell addresses Parliament on 9 December 1644 in a speech that I find both moving and inspiring.

> [T]hat it was now a time, or for ever to hold the tongue. … If I may speak my Conscience without reflection upon any, I do conceive if the army be not put into another Method, and the War more vigorously prosecuted, the people can bear the War no longer, and will enforce you to a dishonourable Peace. But this I would recommend to your Prudence not to insist upon any complaint or Oversight of any Commander in Chief upon any occasion whatsoever; for as I must acknowledge myself guilty of Oversights, so I know they can rarely be avoided in Military Affairs; therefore waving a strict inquiry into the Causes of these things, let us apply our selves to the Remedy which is most necessary: And I hope, we have such true English Hearts, and zealous Affections towards the General Weal of our Mother-Country, as no Members of either House will scruple to deny themselves and their own private interests for the Public Good, nor account to be a dishonour done to them whatever the Parliament shall resolve upon this weighty matter. (Cromwell, 1644)

The bit is now firmly between his teeth; Cromwell continues and makes another two speeches that same day. Parliament listens attentively. The result of which is that two pieces of legislation are tabled. Debates followed by votes take place, all with the objective of getting them on to the statue book. These are the *Self Denying Ordnance* and the *New Model Army Ordinance*. The new year brings success: on 17 February the *New Model Army Ordinance* establishes the new army and its financing and is followed by the *Self Denying Ordinance* on 3 April. This is an important development, as it prevents any Lord or MP from serving in both a government and military capacity. They must relinquish one or the other. Essex is war-weary and too disillusioned to resist Parliament taking away his powers one by one; he resigns on the same day – 3 April 1645. Cromwell, together with a select number of others, with his proven track record on the battlefield and in Parliament is granted an exemption. With command now sanctioned in both Parliament and the army, he is moving towards the moment that will not only define the new model of war but also his position as a leader: the Battle of Naseby.

CHAPTER 5

The Battle of Naseby: The New Model Army's First Engagement, 14 June 1645

1645: a year that made the history books. But despite the passing of two important pieces of legislation in the spring, which effectively put Parliament's military in order, the realities on the ground looked decidedly less promising. The weather in the first months of the year was dominated by heavy rain – not dissimilar to the start of the new year in which I write – which made the movement of troops challenging. At this time, one must remember that there were relatively few roads; they were not much more than tracks and would make our pot-holed roads today look smooth by comparison. This really didn't help the cavalry or even the foot soldiers, both of whom would have been forced to traverse the fields adjacent to the so-called roads. However, the sections that suffered the most were the baggage trains. The baggage trains were, in essence, an early logistics corps. They were responsible for transporting equipment and supplies in carts to where they needed to be, so if they couldn't get to the men who were to fight, there could be little hope of success.

There is an interesting report in *Perfect Occurrences of Parliament* dated Monday 31 March 1645, which reads:

This day there came intelligence from Northampton by Lieutenant General Craford 'Sir,- yesterday being

the Lords day, Lieutenant General Cromwell, being
at this towne of Northampton, with a good body
of Horse and foot by the advice of his Counsell
of Warre, marched from hence with 1500 horse
and two Regiments of foot. To muster at Rugby in
Warwickshire where they intended to quarter that
night about 16 miles march, and after their Muster to
march about 8 or 10 miles further, and there to stay
for the present, to attend towards Coventrie, about 8
or 10 miles further, and there to stay for the present,
to attend the motions of the enemie for the securing
of these parts'. (Crawford, 1645)

I find this fascinating for several reasons. First, it is conclusive
evidence that Cromwell stayed in my constituency, most
probably on 30 March, not long before his long trek to the
defining battle of Naseby. There is an old house in Marefair
sometimes called Cromwell House, and although there is no
evidence that I have seen to support this, I still find it moving
to think of him passing through this, an area I know so well,
with so much expectation. Secondly, the numbers clearly
illustrate the enormity of the task of moving an army around
a country: 1,500 horses and two troops of foot soldiers
navigating over thirty miles of boggy terrain. No mean feat!
But little by little, day by day, the two warring factions, the
royalists and the parliamentarians, were drawing closer to
the battleground.

Sir Thomas Fairfax had been appointed to command the
New Model Army back in January 1645. Cromwell had won

his spurs at Marston Moor when he defeated the royalist right wing, before joining Fairfax for a later skirmish and proving his worth. But he had to wait until the eve of the Battle of Naseby to be promoted. The news of this promotion from Parliament appointing him to be Lieutenant-General of Horse of the Model Army arrives on 5 June and is accepted instantly to the great relief of the general and the whole army. I suppose had Fairfax not been so forthright about his need for Cromwell it might not have happened.

So, what was Cromwell doing in those intervening winter months? The answer: not much, militarily speaking. At this time, due to the inclement weather, as detailed above, armies were forced into winter quarters. However, Cromwell did take three troops of horse to Ely in January, which would have given him an opportunity to see his family.

The clock was ticking and the final countdown had begun. The royalists, led by Prince Rupert, were billeted at Market Harborough and Parliament's at Daventry. Cromwell and the bulk of his cavalry came from East Anglia and rendezvoused at Kislingbury outside Northampton. No one in their right mind would really have chosen the countryside between Naseby where the new Model Army were and East Farndon/ Sibbertoft where the royalists were, yet Providence had other ideas. Fairfax was faced with quite the logistical conundrum in organising his troops – limited by big, high hedges to the west and boggy ground to the east. Added to this were gorse bushes and numerous rabbit holes, so fatal to cavalry. The distance from west to east was about 2,000 yards. The other important element to note was the unequal numbers of troops: parliamentarians had in the region of 7,000 foot soldiers compared to the royalists who had approximately 4,000.

The battle began at 10:00 am.

In the first phase, Prince Rupert's cavalry show promise when they charge and come close to breaking through the parliamentarian cavalry on the west, but they make a mistake: instead of advancing further to support the infantry, they attempt to seize the baggage train. Cromwell, ever observant and quick to react, recognises that the royalist horses on the east side face a really challenging task of trying to charge up a steep slope with rabbit holes everywhere, while being outnumbered. He watches as they struggle then releases his front horse line. Showing no mercy, and with his characteristic impeccable timing, at approximately noon Cromwell releases his second horse line, forcing many of the exhausted royalists to surrender.

Cromwell's actions prove to be decisive. By 1.00 pm the fight has gone so badly for the royalists that they are now in full retreat. Fairfax cleverly restrains the pursuit and follows with Horse and Foot together. The parliamentarians drive the royalists back to Moot Hill but some of them retreat even further to Wadborough, only to be pursued by Cromwell and the Parliamentary Horse.

By mid-afternoon even the King is tempted to join the fight by leading his Lifeguard in a final charge, but his senior officers restrain him to ensure he leaves the battlefield. They want him to head for Market Harborough, a safe ground for royalists, or even to Leicester. Fairfax and Cromwell are not troubled about the King's return to Leicester as they know Sir John Gell, the forceful commander in Derbyshire, would block his retreat to anywhere else to the north.

Soon, the royalist baggage train has been cut off, making escape impossible. Despite being fewer in number in terms of fighting men and horses, the royalist camp had a large accompanying entourage, perhaps indicative of the excesses of court. This included servants as well as a significant number of women, referred to later by a 'Gentleman in Northampton' as the 'middle sort of ammunition, whores full of money and rich apparel maybe as many as 1500'. Many of these poor souls were just slain by the advancing parliamentarian foot soldiers, who no doubt viewed them as collateral damage, purging the court of its excess. It is little wonder, therefore, that the royalist officers were so keen to see the King taken to safety. That said, it could also be argued that not all parliamentarian soldiers were mindless mobsters, as a report in *The Moderate Intelligencer* (12–19 June 1645) clearly shows; some still had respect for the monarch:

> The King in person being necessitated, with his own troop only, to charge through the body for his escape and it is said that his flight was aided by 'a gentleman of the bedchamber; that stood next to the King, and cryed, "hold your hands the King will yield his person" which while they did, he got away'. (*The Moderate Intelligencer*, 1645)

The heat of the battle has passed; the wounded are taken to three churches in Northampton, and the King has retreated to safety – for now. Fairfax, Cromwell and others supporting the parliamentary cause are left to sift through the spoils and along with royalist weapons they find the King's carriage full of private correspondence. In terms of warfare at a strategic level, this is gold. To have access to an enemy's private correspondence is invaluable intelligence and Cromwell and his fellow parliamentarians know this. The 'Naseby Letters', as these documents are called, include secret coded letters between the King and his wife Queen Henrietta. They date from 1641 to 1645 (although most are from 1645). They are quickly taken to London to be deciphered and published later by order of Parliament, as evidence against Charles I in the work *King's Cabinet Opened*.

Secret codes were not new in 1645. In 1586, they had been used in the Babington plot when Mary Queen of Scots planned to assassinate the Protestant Queen Elizabeth I using simple ciphers such as substitution, for example, a = 1. The Naseby letters were more sophisticated, requiring a full-page key, as illustrated in the example shown in the appendix. The Northamptonshire Record Society Library records that frequent uses of a letter like 'a' or 'e' had multiple symbols or numbers and were known as homophonic substitution ciphers. However, what *was* new, or different in 1645, was the increasingly sophisticated use of intelligence. Intelligence meant power, as it provided Parliament with exactly the material it needed to wage a potent campaign of propaganda against the Crown.

At the same time, improvements in printing and rising literacy created fertile ground for this new wave of political messaging. The expanding print trade allowed news and ideas to spread with unprecedented speed.

A wonderful example of this new 'journalism' is evident in more comments from the 'Gentleman in Northampton' who, after touring the battlefield at Naseby, the day after the battle, wrote:

> The Field was about a mile broad where the Battell was fought, and from the outmost Flank of the right, to the left wing took up the whole ground; The bodies lay slaine about four miles in length, the most thicke on the hill the Kings men stood on; I cannot think there was few lesse than four hundred men slaine, and truly I think not many more, and neere 300 horses; Wee tooke at least four thousand Prisoners on the ground between Naseby and Harborough, neere three hundred carriges, whereof twelve of them were Ordnance... There was many wagons laden with rich plunder and others with Arms and Ammunition (*The Kingdomes Weekly Intelligencer*, 1645).

There follows an appendix entitled '414 – RELICS OF NASEBY FIGHT', listing a collection of armour and other antiquarian objects to be sold (see Appendices). I imagine they could only be a small part of the whole and illustrate another unattractive by-product of war: profiteering.

Cromwell remains in the battlefield for the last years of the war, hardly able to attend Parliament, except for a week in

April 1646 – a full ten months after the Battle of Naseby. The intervening period was spent largely with Fairfax and the Model Army dealing with a number of royalist hotspots. These were mainly in the west country and included the taking of Wiltshire, Dorset, Somerset, Devon and Cornwall, culminating with the siege of Oxford in May/June 1646, which resulted in the surrender of the royalists. However, despite the list of parliamentarian wins reading like the Saturday score-draws, life was not that simple. The King had escaped and given himself up to the Scots. They, in turn, held him at Holdenby House in Northamptonshire.

During this time as a full-time soldier, I feel certain that Cromwell would have greatly missed Parliament and his work as an MP: both to represent his Cambridge constituents, who had not seen him for quite a long time, as well as to progress matters of greater national importance. In addition, we know from the Putney Debates his genuine concern for the welfare of the ordinary soldier having experienced the brutality of the battlefield himself. After the Battle of Naseby Cromwell sent a letter to the Speaker of the House of Commons that perfectly reflects his dedication to the cause, his concern for his fellow soldiers and his awareness of the power of language. At a time when printed news and political commentary were reaching wider audiences than ever before, I believe Cromwell's own correspondence carried real weight and authority. He combined his own personal military experience with his devout faith, his words showing the same conviction as his actions on the battlefield. His language is clear and purposeful, offering Parliament a steady narrative at a moment when written language and propaganda were becoming powerful weapons in the battlefield of politics.

> Honest men served you faithfully in this action, Sir, they are trusty; I beseech you in the name of God, not to discourage them. I wish this action may beget thankfulness and humility in all that are concerned in it. He that ventures his life for the liberty of his country, I wish he trust God for the liberty of his conscience and you for the liberty he fights for. (Cromwell, 1645)

CHAPTER 6

An Unholy Trinity of Challenges: Parliament, the Army and the King

With the surrender of royalist Oxford and the flight of King Charles I to join the Scots, the summer of 1646 allows Cromwell to step away from active military service to return to civilian life as an MP. Despite the Self-Denying Ordinance, Cromwell, with his exemption, finds himself in the unique position of holding offices as both army general and active politician. Today, we would call the Self-Denying Ordinance a ruling to prevent conflicts of interest, and I have no doubt it was instigated with that objective in mind. In many ways, the next few years proved especially difficult for Cromwell *because* of his multiple roles, and I feel a degree of frustration on his behalf.

His first action, however, is to move his family from Ely to London's Drury Lane – in those days a residential area with plenty of greenery, which not only shows his commitment to his family, but more importantly his commitment to the parliamentary cause. Later, in 1647, he moves again to King Street in Westminster itself (no longer there) demonstrating, quite literally, his desire to be right in the thick of parliamentary action. At this point, Cromwell had been away from Parliament for four years – almost the equivalent of what today would be a full parliamentary term. Some of his former colleagues would have died; others with whom he had worked previously would be no longer present but, because of the war, would have been replaced by new MPs returned in 'recruiter' elections. However, due to his fighting years across large swathes of the country, when he returns to Westminster, Cromwell is not only known but also respected as a man who doesn't shy away from making tough decisions.

Despite the challenges, given Cromwell's previous experience as an active MP it does not take him long to get restarted as a senior politician and MP. Perhaps a little ironically, one of the most pressing matters that Cromwell finds Parliament is debating on his return is the future of the army. Cromwell wants to stay close to General Fairfax, his former boss, and keeps him updated on parliamentary debates. He sends letters to Fairfax, based in Saffron Waldon – one at the end of July and another dated 8 August 1646. In the August letter, Cromwell reports on developments on the 'Newcastle Propositions', consisting of the Nineteen Propositions of 1642 together with the obligations entered into by the Solemn League and Covenant with Scots (1643). These had been sent by Parliament to the King who had been in Scottish custody since May. The King rejects the Propositions just two days after receiving them, which sent a very powerful message back to Parliament: he would not negotiate. I believe that the King would see negotiation of any kind as weakness. However, Charles's hard stance would certainly have cemented Cromwell's own beliefs that absolute power should not rest with a monarch and continued to fuel his ambition.

Perhaps Charles already knew what I also know as a senior politician and Cromwell was yet to find out: issues are never black and white but always complex. Cromwell had returned from an actual battlefield where strategy and planning worked and battlelines were clearly defined. Now he faced a political battlefield fraught with differences of opinion and conflicting ideologies even if the ultimate objectives, to reduce and restrict the power of the monarch, were the same. Cromwell found himself drawn into ever-more complex debates where battlelines were blurred. It is little wonder that by the end of the year he is taken ill.

As soon as he recovers, in the spring of 1647, he finds he has to defend the army from being disbanded. Many ordinary people, Presbyterians and particularly activists in the City with a very long petition, were pressing for this. Soon after, on 28 April, there was a vote in the House of Commons on the future of the monarchical constitution. Despite all the debate around the need for change, it seems that the House of Commons was not brave enough to push it through: the King's loyalists won 165 to 99 thereby confirming that the monarchical constitution was not to be altered.

I sympathise with Cromwell at the sheer scale and complexity of problems facing him as a senior back bencher who, driven by his conscience, must always take an active interest. He could not and would not copy the King's example of instantly dismissing a notion because it was too fraught with difficulties to address but he must have felt let down by his fellow parliamentarians who voted against a constitutional change.

In my fifty years in politics, the only thing that comes close to the complexity of this situation is when I was deputy speaker and chairman of Ways and Means and I chaired the debates on the Maastricht Bill to take the UK out of the European Union. There were more than 500 amendments all in order to a four-clause Bill, which took twenty-five days, including several all-night sessions, to be debated.

Even though the vote had been taken, debates continued to rumble and rage for months after. Just looking at the long list of dates recorded in the parliamentary records shows how important this topic was: 15 and 16 May, 16 and 17 July, 29 October to 1 November and then 2 to 11 November. Running almost concurrently are the Putney Debates of October to November 1647. Knowing how much preparation and reading there is to be done for any debate in Parliament, my mind spins when I read these dates and the work that must have been involved to keep abreast with them.

The Putney Debates took place in St Mary's Church in Putney, at the time a small riverside village, now familiar to the entire British nation due to it being the starting place of the annual Oxford–Cambridge Boat Race. But it was significant even at the time, too; holding debates about the army and its role in a country amidst the flux of civil unrest in a house of God would have only added to Cromwell's cause. I visited St Mary's and as I stood in the chancel I reflected on Cromwell chairing these debates with all his religious conviction. Not content with being an MP and a military leader, I imagine he saw himself as a religious leader too, driven in his vision to do God's work.

In my research for this book, I have sifted through many pages of internal army debate reflecting the differing attitudes of one regiment to another. Cromwell played an active role all round in trying to unify them all. On 16 May 1646, at the army headquarters in Saffron Walden, Cromwell debates two pressing issues: pay and who should go to Ireland. He deploys his considerable skill in rhetoric to persuade his fellow soldiers to unite: 'Namely to worke in them a good opinion of that authority that is over both "us" and "Them". If that falls to nothing, nothing can follow but confusion. ... I shall desire that you will be pleased to lay this to heart that I have said' (Cromwell, 1646).

Cromwell then has to listen to twenty-two more excitable speeches from leaders of different regiments, all on the same subjects: the structure and pay of the army.

Cromwell continues to debate and petition on behalf of the army in Westminster but, by June, he decides to quit Westminster, I think through frustration, and heads to Saffron Walden to deal with the army's leaders 'in person'. His mission is to dissuade the New Model Army from confronting Parliament directly. He is able to inform them that Parliament has agreed to grant indemnity and pay arrears, which not only shows his skill at negotiating but would have also helped maintain – and elevate – his own reputation within the military. Today, we are all used to seeing politicians 'out and about' making visits and speeches to key voters and business leaders, followed by an entourage from the press. But, in the sixteenth century, this would have been new, and I like to think that Cromwell understood this: that face-to-face meetings were infinitely better than relying on reports sent out from Westminster.

I remember all too clearly a challenge I faced as the new MP for Northampton South after the two elections of 1974. Northampton had been designated a fourth-generation 'New Town', which gave sweeping powers to the Development Corporation much to the disgust of both the Town and County Councils. It was clear to me that Northampton Borough, in effect all my constituency and most of neighbouring Northampton North, had no choice but to work with the Development Corporation. I had had the experience of being leader of the London Borough of Islington for three years from 1969 to 1971 so had a good understanding of how governance at a local level worked.

I took it upon myself to be the informal liaison between the Northampton councils and the Development Corporation, informing all parties what and why I was taking this role, which, off the record, at the time, I cleared with the relevant Secretary of State. I realised we could not alter the decision but, if we were astute, I could ensure that the Development Corporation both listened to the local concerns and listened to any extra propositions I raised.

It worked. Out of it came new investment, such as the creation of the University of Northampton (today near the top of the second-division universities), new inward investment in industry and trade, a new railway station, and an increasingly positive mix of both social and owner occupation.

Back to Cromwell. However, while he is busy negotiating between army and Parliament, the third element in this unhappy trinity, the King, also demands his attention. On the night of 2/3 June, a body of the New Model Horse, led by Cornet Joyce, arrived at Holmby House (Holdenby House) in Northamptonshire where the King was being held. Having originally been taken there by the Scots, the King has now been turned over to the army. Joyce takes the King towards Newmarket where most of the New Model Army are stationed and, on 7 June, Cromwell comes to Childerley, near his constituency of Cambridge, to meet the King. His response to the monarch is lukewarm, as he worries about the King's real intentions.

Cromwell stays close to the army headquarters as he and other generals draft their own constitutional settlement entitled *Heads of the Proposals*. Signed by Skippon, Ireton, Fleetwood and Cromwell, this is delivered to the House of Commons by Cromwell. It is in part a response to the continued call for the disbandment of the New Model Army by key figures in London, including the Lord Mayor, Aldermen and Common Council of the City of London. (Although, they soon had to think again when their own trained bands supported the army.) Coupled with this, Cromwell is aware of rumours that the Scots are being troublesome and tensions are rising in favour of the absent monarch.

Perhaps with this growing tension both between and within the army and Westminster, and with the army settled at Saffron Walden, it is not surprising that Cromwell makes what turns out to be his final speech in Westminster on 3 January 1648. The debate concerned the latest attempt for a constitutional settlement, no fewer than four Bills, all outright rejected by the King. Cromwell urges the House to stand firm. In his view it is the King who has broken trust, who 'owns not a God', and who has dragged out the war. Little could Cromwell have known as he sat down that he would not speak again in Parliament until 6 January 1649. In the meantime, he would be occupied elsewhere, writing and sending no fewer than seventythree formal letters to the Speaker and others in authority.

This political stalemate, the intricate and complicated to-ing and fro-ing between military and Westminster is forced to a temporary halt with the arrival of some dramatic news. The adjutant-general in Wales, Fleming, has been killed in a royalist uprising. The decision was made to send Cromwell with a large force to Wales to deal with the uprising. He would have felt morally fortified by the resolution of the army: 'It was our duty, if ever the Lord brought us back again in peace to call Charles Stuart, that man of blood, to account for the blood he had shed, and mischief he had done' (Army resolution, 1648).

So, Cromwell finds himself back in the saddle yet again, this time to carry out the important work: 'to subdue' a royalist uprising and prevent a second civil war. His first stop was Gloucester where he addresses his troops. He must have been acutely aware that it had been two years since he and the troops under his command had physically fought against the enemy led by Charles Stuart, 'that man of blood'. Two years older but also two years wiser: he is now a prominent leader, an excellent orator and he treats his men to a rousing, motivating speech in the style of his best in the House of Commons. The speech is peppered with the language of unity and shared experience: 'he had often times ventured his life with them and they with him', and later calling for 'the same courage, faithfulness and fidelity', finishing with the words 'for his part, he protested to live and die with them'. The reception was reported as outstanding with 'a great shout and hallow' – caps thrown in the air as testament to total commitment to General Cromwell.

This time, the enemy was not just the royalists but also a defector called Colonel Poyer and his Presbyterian followers. They were no push over for Cromwell and presented a viciousness and brutality not found before. They were really anti-Parliament. Fortunately for Cromwell, a former Parliamentary Commander, Colonel Horton, had already dealt the rebels a blow at St Fagans near Cardiff. Cromwell is tasked with dealing with rebel strongholds, which he does successfully, eventually reaching Cardiff and then moving on to Tenby Castle, which capitulates after a week. This just leaves Pembroke Castle, the strongest castle in Wales. Cromwell has to lay a siege as he has no real firepower to demolish any of the walls, and much to his surprise it takes nearly two months before they surrender.

Cromwell sends a letter to Speaker Lenthall on 18 July 1648 about the eventual surrender at Pembroke, which clearly shows that he now understood the conflict in explicitly religious terms. He writes that he 'did rather make election of them, than those who had always been for the king, judging their iniquity double because they have sinned against so many evidences of divine presence' (Cromwell, 1648). Effectively, he is arguing that royalists were not just politically mistaken but spiritually at fault. In his view, they had persisted in supporting the king despite what he saw as repeated signs of God's favour towards Parliament. Their guilt was therefore 'double': they had chosen the wrong side, and they had done so in defiance of providence. It's a revealing moment, showing how Cromwell's interpretation of the war had shifted from a political struggle to a moral and religious one.

I do think that in many ways Cromwell's military appointment was detrimental to his political responsibilities as a Member of Parliament, as while he was away fighting on the battlefield, Parliament would continue to sit and debate the machinations of the issues of the day. It makes me wonder why his military responsibilities could not have been shared with Ireton allowing him to come back to Westminster regularly not only to report firsthand on the action at the frontline but also to continue to participate in debate.

Perhaps one way to look at it is that Cromwell is a victim of his own military success. Having 'sorted out' Wales he receives orders to go to the North of England to help Lord Lambert who is facing an imminent attack from the Scots. This they duly did on 8 July, just three days before the surrender of

Pembroke Castle. This Scottish army of 'Engagers' is led by the Duke of Hamilton, supported by the King, together with more extreme Presbyterians.

Cromwell, no doubt weary from the fighting in Wales, now faces appalling weather conditions too and only reaches Doncaster on 8 August. Even after joining forces with Lambert's troops, the Parliamentarians still only have a total of 8,500 men compared to the Scottish force of approximately 21,000. This is not the book to go into detail of the Battle of Preston. Suffice to say the Scots' leadership made one bad decision after another resulting in their total defeat with two generals captured and the third escaping to France. The casualty figures tell enough of the story. The number of Scots killed totals 2,000; Cromwell's men, less than a hundred. Another letter is dispatched to the Speaker of the House and afterwards it was printed as a pamphlet, so impressive and rousing were its contents. Cromwell speaks rapturously of the hand of God, further evidence of his religious conviction and his belief. I must say it must and should have gone down well with other MPs, but the reverse happened as the Commons deliberately repealed the 'Vote of No Addresses to the King'. Essentially, this paved the way to reopen negotiations with the King and Cromwell would have seen it as a step backwards at the very moment when the war's meaning seemed most stark. The Second Civil War had confirmed to Cromwell that Charles could not be trusted and that God's judgement had already been shown on the battlefield. Parliament's decision to resume talks therefore looked not only politically naïve but spiritually misguided, ignoring what he believed were unmistakable signs of divine direction. But if Cromwell felt frustrated by this, he would have felt even more alienated from Parliament in the month that followed.

On 12 September 1648 Cromwell was ordered to recover the two border fortresses of Berwick and Carlisle and then enter Scotland, which he did on 21 September. The new leader in Scotland was Archibald Campbell, the 1st Marquess of Argyll who seemed to support a new type of Scottish patriotism. Cromwell met the new leaders with whom, as sincere Calvinists, he had much in common. On Wednesday 4 October Cromwell, Lambert and other army leaders were invited to Edinburgh, welcomed by the Marquess of Argyll 'as deliverer of their country'. The visit lasted three days, culminating with a special dinner held in Edinburgh Castle. This must have been a welcome change from the bloodshed of the battlefield and I do wonder if Cromwell, despite his Puritan beliefs, did allow himself to enjoy the pomp and pageantry of a state dinner. He certainly uses the occasion to his political advantage by seeking to secure the exclusion of all 'Engagers' from offices of trust. Cromwell must have negotiated effectively, because on 6 October the Scottish leader Loudon reported that there was full agreement on all of Cromwell's terms, including the disbandment of Monro's army. Yet even with this apparent consensus, many in Scotland still held firmly to the idea of a distinct Scottish nation – a sentiment that, as we know, continues to be felt by many today.

But while Cromwell and the army were enjoying the fruits of their successes in Scotland, Westminster continued to operate on its own agenda. Much to the disgust of the military, Parliament had followed up the repeal of the Vote of No Addresses with another application to the King who came up with the suggestion of a three-year experiment. This was rejected but I am sure that Cromwell and the Scottish leadership would have had strong opinions on it.

On 9 October Cromwell reported to the Speaker of the Commons that all Scotland's forces were now disbanded. Unfortunately, there were still patches of dissent in the North that needed sorting out, particularly Pontefract Castle. This took another eight weeks with the result that Cromwell missed all the discussions, conferences, Councils' proposals and counterproposals while he was stuck with military matters. He must have felt frustrated and that he was out of the politics game – a long way from London, both literally and metaphorically. In all honesty, I do not understand why, after his success in Edinburgh, he did not appoint a deputy so that he could head to Westminster as a senior MP to support Parliament in its time of real need.

CHAPTER 7

'Liberty! Freedom! Tyranny is Dead!':[*]
The Trial and Execution of Charles I

When he hears of the King's arrival, Cromwell hastens to the window and watches him as he comes up through the gardens. This is Westminster, in mid-winter, and the gardens would be sparse and bare yet ordered and quiet – the perfect space to reflect on the enormity of the moment. Cromwell had been fighting for constitutional change for years; to his mind Charles with his belief that it was his 'Divine Right' to be king was the very embodiment of a tyrannical, autocratic ruler. It must have felt strange to see the King as a mere mortal, walking across the cotton garden in Westminster. The moment was certainly not lost on Cromwell who was reported to turn 'white as the wall.' Turning away, he drew together Bradshaw, Sir Henry Mildmay and Sir William Brereton and is believed to have said: 'My Masters, he is come, he is come, and now we are doing that great work that the whole nation will be full of.' (Fraser 1973: 344 citing C.V. Wedgwood).

How right he was. This was the culmination of years of conflict: personal, political, national. Much blood had been spilled; communities divided; lives lost. Wars had been

____

[*] from Shakespeare's *Julius Caesar*, after Caesar is killed

76

fought in England's fields and in her courthouses. After such a tumultuous period, Cromwell must have felt enormous relief that the King had been brought to Westminster without trouble or demonstration. I cannot help but think about when I too, as Michael Morris MP in my role as first deputy speaker and chairman of Ways and Means, had an office that overlooked the gardens in Westminster. They provided many a moment of quiet reflection away from the noise of the House.

Cromwell, having only arrived in London on 6 December, a few short weeks before, snaps out of his reverie. There is work to be done and quickly, too. He asks his companions: 'Therefore I desire ye to let us resolve here what answer we shall give the King when he comes before us, for the first question that he will ask us will be by what authority and commission do we try him' then a quick-witted Marten who said, 'In the name of the Commons and Parliament assembled and all the good people of England' (Fraser 1973 citing C. V. Wedgwood).

*

The leaders of the army had been discussing their draft of a Remonstrance since 7 November. By this point the army was not just a fighting machine but a political force of its own, suspicious of Westminster following Parliament's decision to repeal the Vote of No Addresses. Much discussion had taken place and, largely thanks to the work of Henry Ireton, a final draft of this Remonstrance was tabled on 16 November. It was then presented to the Commons on the twentieth, taking four hours to be delivered.

Crucially, Cromwell had been kept out of Westminster during these debates, as he was fighting in Scotland to subdue any remaining royalists. He remembers the letter he sent to Fairfax broadly supporting some of the petitions without really thinking what might be the outcome. Indeed, he wrote: 'I find in the Officers of the Regiments a very great sense of the sufferings of this poor Kingdom; and in them all a very great zeal to have impartial Justice done upon Offenders; and I verily think and am persuaded they are things which God puts into our hearts' (Morrill, 2022).

The Commons clearly realise there is a growing head of steam in the army's Remonstrance; there is a strong demand for the dissolution of this Parliament allied to a desire for a much more democratic system of election. Parliament tries to buy itself time, a common tactic when an issue is really complicated, and takes a week to consider the Remonstrance. I imagine Parliament was hoping and praying that the King might just understand the seriousness of the situation and enter into meaningful dialogue at this point. But Charles could only understand absolutes: to his mind, he had been chosen by God and therefore could not contemplate the permanent abolition of the episcopacy where Church and its leaders were compulsory in the ruling mix. Charles's failure to compromise left the Commons adrift in mid-stream: they wanted to engage in dialogue with the monarch, but he simply could not.

On 27 November, the Commons decided to once again adjourn discussion on the Remonstrance. The situation was becoming impossible. However, at the same time, the General Council at Windsor decided the Army should move to London. Perhaps this was the move needed to break the stalemate. The Commons moved and finally voted on the Remonstrance and rejected it: 125 votes to 58.

The army is incensed. This is proof that Parliament is still entertaining the idea of negotiating with the King, a notion completely abhorrent to the military leaders who have seen so much blood shed on the battlefield in the name of their cause. The army react in the way it knows best: with a show of military strength. Soldiers march on London and pitch camp in Hyde Park. The King and his supporters seemed unmoved by this very public show of aggression, but tensions are mounting: the next morning, London awakes to find Parliament surrounded by military guard. It is time for the army to launch its attack.

Step forward Colonel Thomas Pride, an officer who had fought at the Battle of Naseby. In his hand is a list of MPs to be debarred as proscribed by the army. Some Members simply turned away but those who resisted were locked up together in a chamber. The net result of this purge, later to be known as Pride's Purge, was to leave the House of Commons with just about eighty members and, crucially, only those who would vote to get rid of the King.

The following day, 9 December 1648, Oliver Cromwell returns to the House of Commons and takes his seat as an MP. He has been absent for seven months. His return is welcomed by the *sotto voce* rumble from Members, coupled with a congratulatory speech from Sir Henry Vane. Understandably the remaining Members want their presence to be recognised but it is a challenge to even get a quorum of forty. Alongside these parliamentary hostilities the general public are pretty hostile, too.

Over the following three weeks, Cromwell is tasked to organise the Trial of the King. He has a proven track record of administrating thorny issues and none more so than this. The votes in favour of the King's response to the Newport Proposals are annulled and a new 'Agreement of the people' is debated. Cromwell only takes a part-time role in this; no doubt the logistics of the trial take up a lot of time. The King is brought to Windsor Castle and is heavily guarded.

The army is clear that under no circumstances will the King's life be spared. On the surface, Cromwell's position is less clear. In the weeks leading up to the trial he was not as openly vociferous as the military leaders but personally I feel this was simply because he was so consumed with procedural processes. Following his experiences of fighting in the recent Second Civil War, his rhetoric had certainly changed; he felt betrayed by Charles, that he could not be trusted, and that he, Cromwell, was fulfilling God's work to purge the nation of a tyrannical, treacherous ruler. I personally cannot see him having a message from God to spare the life of the King who had initiated two major wars resulting in thousands being killed.

On 28 December things begin to move as the House of Commons read for the first time the Ordinance to set up a special court for the trial of the King. This was passed on 1 January 1649. Cromwell had done his homework. However, the much-diminished House of Lords rejects the court, primarily on the grounds that there was no machinery for the trial of a King. The House of Commons react and push through a new Act passed on 6 January, which gives it sole responsibility for the court. However, one must recognise that among ordinary people there was no conviction that this was the right course of action. Nevertheless, the momentum is by now in full swing; soon after the Chief Justice of Cheshire, John Bradshaw, is chosen to be president of the court and then work starts to draft the charge to be brought against the King who must also be brought to London.

20 January 1649: the scene is now set for the formal trial of the King of England, Charles I, to take place in Westminster Hall. An imposing and unique building constructed by William Rufus after 1066, to this day it continues to have a special aura of solemnity. Over the half century that I have been attending Westminster, I often pause on the steps at the north end to take a moment to reflect on this momentous event – an event that shaped the democratic systems we continue to enjoy today and in which Cromwell played a vital part. At the time of Charles's trial, Westminster Hall was already instrumental in the judicial system and home to the law courts, including the King's Bench, the Chancery, and the Court of the Exchequer. Galleries could be constructed for major occasions such as

this as they are today. Indeed, there is a brass plate marking the very spot where King Charles sat for his trial.

For all his faults, Charles always had a presence and dignity in his bearing. This occasion was no different. He refused to remove his hat, reflecting his view that the whole procedure was illegal. Sadly, we do not know where Cromwell was seated exactly within the three rows of judges, but my guess is at one of the ends of the front row. Soon after my arrival in both the House of Commons and the House of Lords, I learned that if one wants to be noticed, the end of a row is the place to be. Interestingly, not all of Cromwell's military associates were as committed as he was. One notable example was General Fairfax who Cromwell would have expected to be present but was not. I have thought about this and can only assume that despite an exemplary military record of fighting for a cause they passionately believed in, some must have felt overwhelmed by the magnitude of this occasion. By the same token, credit must be given to those, including Cromwell, who did have the bravery and conviction to attend. The charge was then read by John Cook, solicitor, as the Attorney General had 'conveniently' pleaded illness, further proof that this task was not for the faint-hearted.

The King listened and tried to interrupt but to no avail. The main lines of the charge were the same as the Act of 6 January, that he was 'a tyrant, traitor, murderer and a public and implacable enemy of the Commonwealth of England'. He had levied war against Parliament and been 'the author of the second war'.

Charles's response was as expected. He questioned the authority that had brought the charges against him and was told firmly that it had been brought by the people of England. The King maintained he was not a subject within the Common Law of England and, as he refused to enter a plea, the clerk was told to 'record his default'. The trial continues and, on 25 January, there is some attempt to present an objective court by the calling of witnesses. However, all substantiate that the King had fought and levied war against his people, resulting in the forty-six men present ruling that the court should now proceed directly to the sentencing of the accused: Charles Stuart.

In acknowledgement of the severity of the proceeding, some felt they needed even more than forty-six, so a further sixteen MPs, with either a legal or parliamentary background, were recruited, making sixty-two. The new sentence made no mention of high treason but stated that Charles should be 'put to death by the severing of his head from his body'. By the following morning, Friday 26 January 1649, fifty-nine men, including Pride, Ireton, Okey and Waller had all signed the death warrant. Cromwell's signature was third on the list. I have seen it myself – a clear testament to Cromwell's conviction. Further proof is that Cromwell, ever the politician, sets to work chasing up the missing three colleagues to add their signatures. In politics, this is known as 'whipping' and Cromwell was an expert. This signed document used to hang in the 'No' Lobby in the House of Commons for all to see. I do not know who took the decision to remove it, but I think it should be returned to its position to remind all MPs of the importance of the trial leading to our Parliamentary Democracy of today.

On Saturday 27 January, Charles is brought back to Westminster Hall to hear the sentence against him read out accompanied by cries from soldiers of 'Justice' and 'Execution!' Charles tries to intervene but fails as the clerk reads the formal sentence followed by Bradshaw who takes it upon himself to remind those present of the previously deposed or decapitated sovereigns, including Edward III, Richard II and Mary Queen of Scots.

Appeals to Cromwell came from overseas seeking mercy. Louis XIV of France personally wrote a strongly worded letter, pleading for the King's life and another letter was received from the States-General of the Netherland. But to no avail and, so, the dirty business of preparing for an execution starts. Scaffolding is erected in front of the highly decorated Banqueting House; the balcony remains even today for all to see and reflect upon.

Tuesday 30 January 1649: the day of execution arrives. Charles Stuart walks with calm dignity from St James's Palace to the scaffold in Whitehall. At 2 pm precisely he steps forth from the Banqueting House on to the balcony accompanied by his chaplain, Bishop Juxon. Two Colonels are in charge of proceedings not least to prevent any last-minute appeals to the large crowd assembled below. But a minute later the executioner holds up the severed head with the traditional cry of, 'Behold the head of a traitor.' Charles Stuart is dead. England has overthrown her constitutional Head.

Cromwell is not present at the King's death. Instead, he attends a prayer meeting in the House of Commons and waits for the news to come via a messenger. On receipt of the news, he orders for the King's body to be buried quickly. Cromwell's reaction to the execution of Charles I was entirely in keeping with his character and beliefs. As a devout Puritan who believed his war against Charles had been fulfilling God's will, it was natural to turn to prayer at such a decisive and significant moment. Although stories circulated that Cromwell's secretary visited the king's coffin, these tales lack evidence and I myself do not believe them. A year later, while in Edinburgh, Cromwell described the king's death in a letter to Hammond as 'the great fruit of the war', calling it 'the execution of exemplary justice upon the prime leader of this quarrel' (Morrill, 2022). Throughout his life, when confronted by royalists and later critics, Cromwell consistently maintained–correctly in my view–that 'Providence and necessity', under the guidance of the Lord, had directed his actions.

CHAPTER 8

The Commonwealth: 1649–1653

Following Charles's death, England became a Commonwealth, and I have pondered on the choice of that word. England could have been called a Republic. Both denote countries that do not have a monarch so either could have been chosen. The *Oxford English Dictionary*'s definition of Commonwealth is: 'The public welfare and general good meaning of the new body politic or the state, especially viewed as a body in which the whole people had a voice or interest.' Historical examples of Republics, which would have been known to Cromwell, included Venice and of course Rome. In the seventeenth century, however, the closest Republic to England, geographically speaking, was the Dutch Republic, which was also well-known to Cromwell and posed a threat. Perhaps the idea of a Republic felt too foreign, too radical. It is important to remember that in overthrowing a monarch and a constitutional system that had been in operation for centuries, the people of England must have been holding their breath, waiting to see what would happen next. Also, continued civil unrest would be a real threat, so I cannot imagine Cromwell, or Parliament, would want to give too much power to the people by naming England a Republic. Cromwell knew that the country needed a firm hand through this turbulent time and he could provide that as a military

Hall Court of Sidney Sussex College, Cambridge, which Cromwell attended in 1616–1617. (Wikimedia Commons)

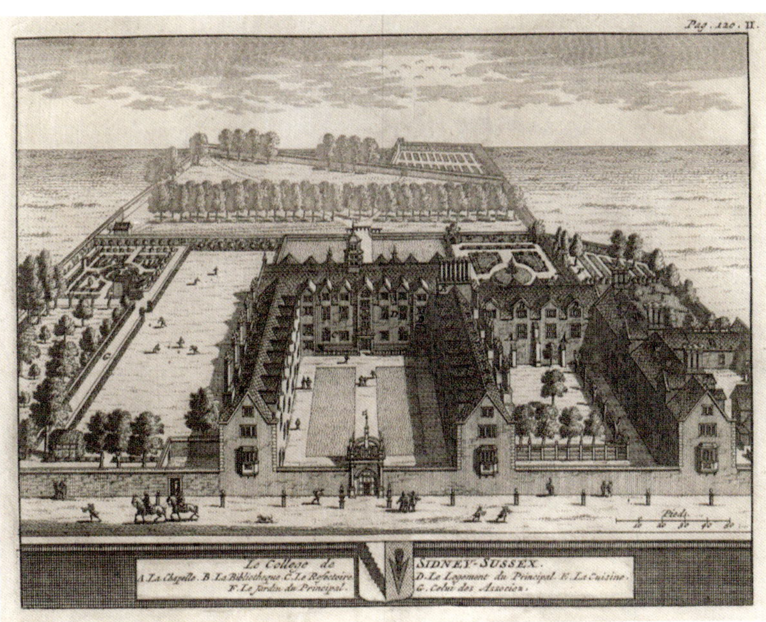

Sidney Sussex College, Cambridge. Engraving by David Loggan, published in 1690. (Chronicle / Alamy)

John Bunyan (1628–1688); Puritan, political thinker and writer whose liberal beliefs led him to be imprisoned in Bedford Gaol for eleven years. (Wikimedia Commons)

The Petition of Right. During the reign of Charles I, there was accelerating political tension concerning the power of Parliament and the 'rights and liberties of the subject'. In 1628 the House of Commons drafted this petition proclaiming, among other things, the illegality of taxation without parliamentary consent and of arbitrary imprisonment. (Parliamentary Archives, HL/PO/PU/1/1627/3C1n2)

Speaker Lenthall Asserting the Privileges of the Commons Against Charles I when the Attempt was made to Seize the Five Members, waterglass painting by Charles West Cope. (Photo courtesy: UK Parliament, WOA 2894)

Photograph of the entrance to the Falcon pub, Huntingdon, *c.*1930. This was where Cromwell raised his first troop of cavalry in 1642; it still looks much the same today. (Courtesy of Huntingdonshire Archives)

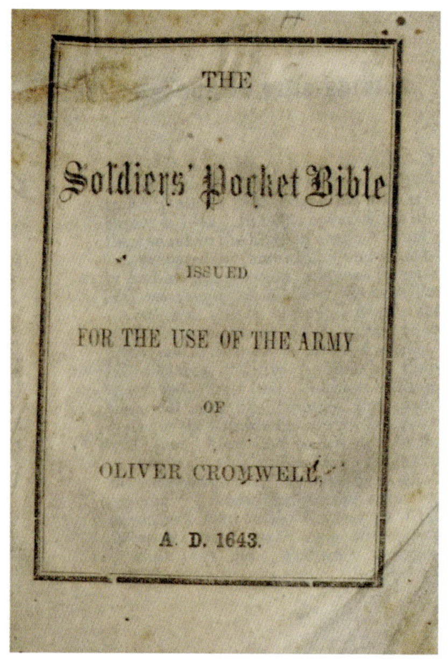

The Soldiers' Pocket Bible.
Issued by Cromwell to every man in his army, in 1643. (Edition 1860 Internet Archive / Duke University Libraries)

Title page of *The Souldiers Pocket Bible*, 1643.
(Wikimedia Commons)

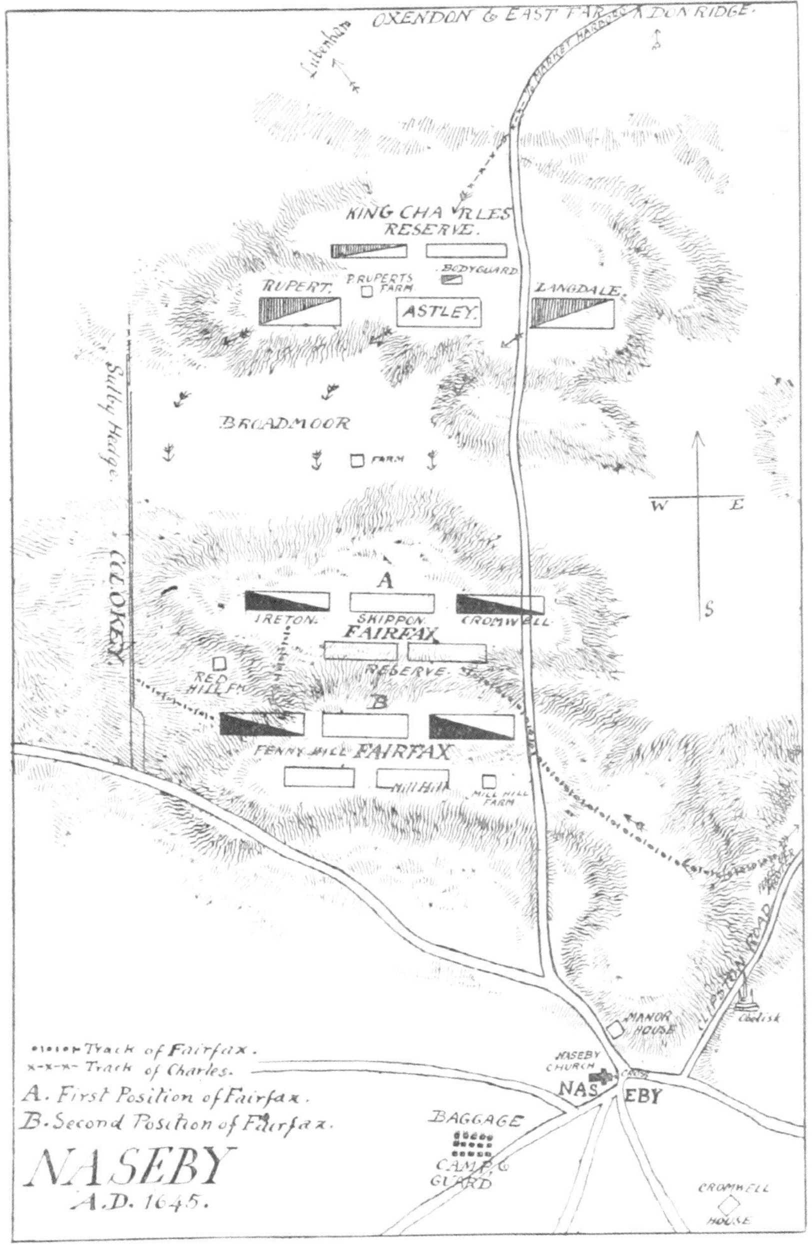

Map detailing the first battle between Parliament's New Model Army and the King's troops: a triumph for Cromwell leading the cavalry. (Wikimedia Commons)

In the Civil War between Charles I. and his Parliament, Northamptonshire played a conspicuous part. The county town was garrisoned for the Parliament, and during the early years of the war numerous skirmishes took place in its vicinity. These are fully described in various letters and tracts of the period ; but even if this were not the case, we should conclude that a good deal of fighting must have taken place in the neighbourhood, from the frequent records of the burial of soldiers in parish registers up and down the county.

Thus in 1642, the feoffees of St. Giles' paid two shillings for the burial of two soldiers ; and again in 1644, five shillings was expended on the burial of "two maimed soldiers."

In June, 1645, the decisive battle of the war was fought at Naseby, 15 miles from Northampton, and many of the wounded who were brought into the town, succumbed to their injuries a few days after the fight.

The registers of St. Sepulchre's and All Saints, Northampton, record the burial of numerous soldiers during the month of June, 1645. Some are mentioned by name, others are described as "soldiers unknown" ; while the rest are summed up in the following comprehensive record (in the register of All Saints) :—

"This month thirty comon soldiers sepult fuit."

The registers of St. Giles', at this date, are almost a blank, but they contain at least one interesting Civil War entry :—

"1645. Sir Tho. Dallison die June ye 20."*

Reference to the wounded of the Battle of Naseby, 1645, being taken to St Sepulchre and St Giles churches, both in the author's parliamentary constituency. (Northamptonshire Archives and Heritage Service)

Church of the Holy Sepulchre, Northampton. The surrounding area, including the churchyard, was a scene of conflict. While the church survived the fighting, records indicate that major repairs were necessitated around this period and many Royalist prisoners were held in the Church itself. (Wikimedia Commons/ David P Howard)

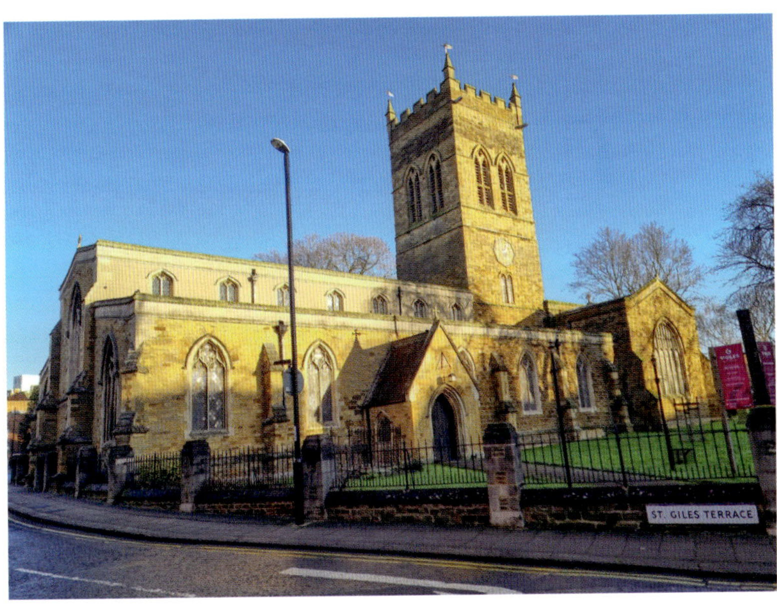

St Giles Church, Northampton. The church features musket ball holes from the period and is located near the medieval town walls and defences. (Wikimedia Commons)

William Lenthall, Speaker of the House of Commons, 1640–60. Painting by Henry Paert. (Photo courtesy: Parliament, Heritage Collections, WOA 2712)

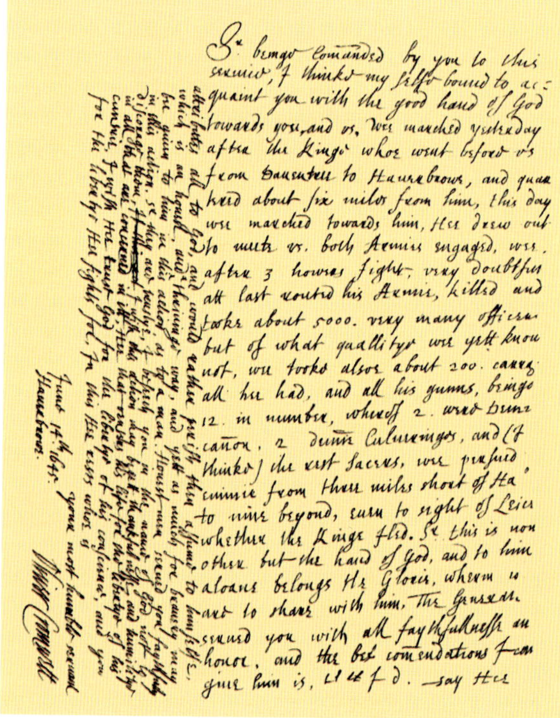

Letter from Oliver Cromwell to William Lenthall, Speaker of the House of Commons, announcing the defeat of the King. (Lebrecht Music & Arts / Alamy)

Engrossment of the Official Record of the Trial or King Charles I.
(Parliamentary Archives, HL/PO/JO/10/14/11A)

Letter from King Charles I to the House of Lords in favour of mercy towards the Earl of Strafford. (Parliamentary Archives, HL/PO/JO/10/1/56A)

Death Warrant of King Charles I, 29 Jan 1649.
(Parliament's archive collections HL/PO/JO/10/1/297A)

The Magna Carta, 1215, was the first written document to show that the King and his government were not above the law and specifically that a government can only last as long as it has the agreement and support of the people. The Magna Carta remains a powerful symbol of liberty around the world today. 1733 engraving by John Pine of the 1215 charter. (Cotton Charter XIII.31A / CBW/Alamy)

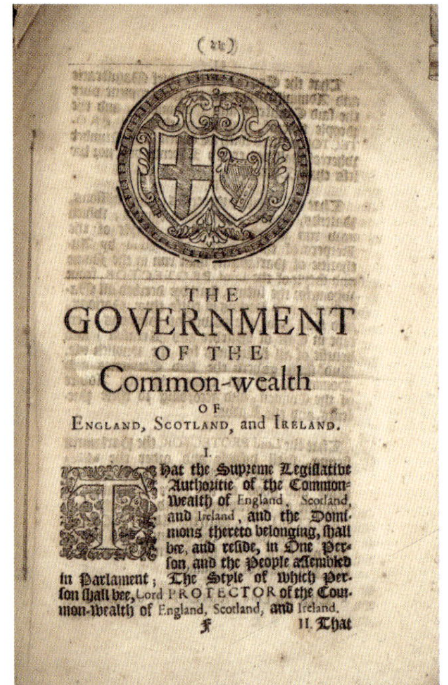

Printed copy of 'The Instrument of Government', 1653. (Courtesy of the Cromwell Museum, Huntingdon, UK)

Engraving showing Cromwell dismissing the Rump Parliament in 1653, from a painting by Benjamin West, 1783. (Courtesy of the Cromwell Museum, Huntingdon, UK)

Castle Sinclair Girnigoe, near Wick, Noss Head, Caithness, Scotland. A typical example of ruins left after one of Cromwell's military campaigns in Scotland. (Arterra Picture Library / Alamy)

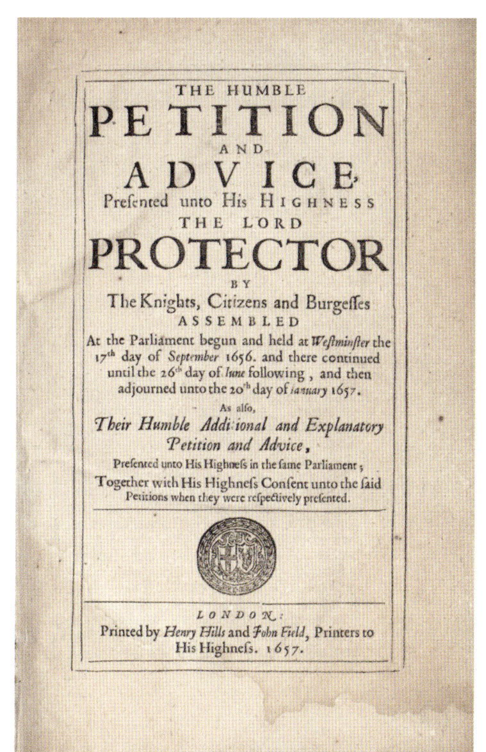

Printed copy of 'The Humble Petition and Advice', 1657. (Courtesy of the Cromwell Museum, Huntingdon, UK)

Oliver Cromwell, circle of Robert Walker, oil on canvas, *c*.1649.
(Courtesy of the Cromwell Museum, Huntingdon, UK)

Extracts from a Commission from Oliver
Cromwell. (Northamptonshire Archives and
Heritage Service W(A)/Box 1/IV/10)

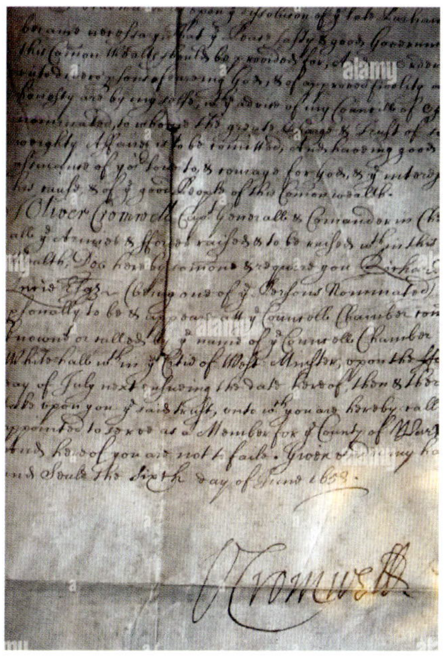

Writ of Summons to the Barebone's Parliament, signed by Oliver Cromwell (1599–1658). In 1653, Cromwell personally nominated members to a new assembly (Parliament) rather than holding elections. Each member received a writ like this requiring them to attend. (Alamy)

Bust of King Charles I located in St Margaret's Church, Westminster, facing Parliament and the statue of Oliver Cromwell, 'for all eternity'.

Oliver Cromwell (1599–1658). Sculpture by Sir William Hamo Thorneycroft. (Photo courtesy: UK Parliament, WOA S29)

Michael Morris, Deputy Speaker of the House of Commons, 1992–1997, in the Speaker's chair.

The author in Westminster Hall at the location of the trial of King Charles I. The plaque reads: The King, Charles Stuart, was tried for high treason on this spot by the High Court of Justice established by the Commons of England for that purpose, Saturday 20th, Monday 22nd, Tuesday 23rd and Saturday 27th January 1649. The King was convicted of treason and sentenced to death on Saturday 27th January and executed in front of the Banqueting House, Whitehall Palace, at two o'clock in the afternoon of Tuesday 30th January 1649.

leader with his faith to guide him. I believe that in making the choice to be a Commonwealth, Cromwell knew that the real power was concentrated in the hands of Parliament. He also knew he was the de facto leader of Parliament. Technically, the abolition of the monarchy was only passed on 17 March 1649, and the Commonwealth itself was not formally enacted until May but what a time it must have been with so many issues to address.

In considering the meaning of a Commonwealth and how a country is governed, I reflect on my own experiences of working in and with countries such as India, Sri Lanka, the Maldives, Singapore, Canada and Australia – not to mention the Overseas Territories, including places like the Falklands. I've often found that the determining common factor is the same: helping and working alongside these nations to support their communities. Whatever the constitutional arrangements or political histories, the real measure of a system lies in how it serves the people who live within it. I like to think that Cromwell understood this and, guided by his faith, did believe in 'public welfare and general good'.

Lofty ideals are all very well, but they take an enormous amount of organisation and work to drive through and never more so than in 1649. The House of Lords was officially abolished on 19 March 1649, which also swept away its judicial function as well. Many of the long-standing organisations and roles were also abolished, such as the Star Chamber, Lord Chancellor and Chancellor of the Exchequer as well as the Privy Council of which I am a proud Member. What remained became known as the Rump Parliament, just 140 MPs who worked together in the House of Commons with a Speaker of the House alongside the new and powerful Council of State. The Council of State was structured to have forty-one members and a quorum of nine members. Elections had taken place on 14 February with Cromwell in the vanguard and elected first acting chairman. He was also chosen to be commander in chief of the Army, which, given the volatile times, could easily be seen as the highest position of all. He soon demonstrated his leadership by being the first to take the oath and saying he felt the new Commonwealth should be supported by the widest possible base. He reminded Members that they were entering a new form of Parliament with implications across the whole country in the appointment of Justices of Peace and the new High Court of Justice. The Council of State was supported by a series of committees – I suppose what we would call Parliamentary Departments today, assigned to different areas of governance and national interest, including Foreign, the Armed Forces and Ireland. Again, this short list belies England's most pressing issues of the day and clearly illustrates the fragility of this new world order, again showing the need for strong leadership.

But there needed to be visible changes for all citizens to see too and this involved the removal of all royal regalia and insignia from public display. This included new coinage and new flags. I find the scale of this operation incredible, especially when I think that, at the time of writing, it has been more than three years since Queen Elizabeth II died and yet, despite it being the twenty-first century and all the technological and logistical wizardry of our age, I still do not see many banknotes with King Charles's portrait on them.

So, England in 1648/9 was forging ahead with its constitutional and practical changes: the new Great Seal depicted a crowded House of Commons complete with Speaker in the Chair with no reference to the House of Lords at all. It was circumscribed 'In the First Year of Freedom by God's blessing 1648'. The Great Seal was the official stamp used to authenticate all acts of governance – laws, Bills, Acts and so forth. Previously, the monarch would have added their seal to these documents, so, with its abolition, it was vital that the ruling powers replaced it quickly. Similarly, the Mace, which was, and still is, a physical and ceremonial symbol of the authority of the House of Commons and sits in the House whenever it is in session, had the following phrase added to it: 'The Commonwealth of England and God with us'.

Such a new organisation needed propaganda in the true meaning of the word to support the raft of constitutional changes. The arrival of the printing press and advances in mass production of printed matter certainly facilitated the wider circulation of key information, as one pamphlet of the day testified: 'Old England now is grown perfectly new and we in another world.' Pamphlets were hugely popular throughout the country at a time when literacy rates were also increasing. It is believed that one in three people could read, so even if an average person couldn't read, the chances are they would know someone who could! In this way, coverage of events at

Westminster and the dissemination of news could quickly cover the whole of the country. In addition, one John Milton, a talented wordsmith and my favourite poet, was on hand to support the Commonwealth and did so with his writing, including a pamphlet with the longest title I have ever come across: The Tenure of Kings and Magistrates: 'Proving that it is lawful, and Hath been Held so through All Ages, for Any, who Have the Power, to call to Account a Tyrant or Wicked King, and after Due Conviction to Depose and put him to death'.

Given all that they had achieved, and in such a short time, I imagine that by late spring of 1649, Cromwell, Ireton and their parliamentary colleagues must have been in a good, confident mood, almost wooing the nation into resignation with their swift sweep of reform. But, at the same time, they must have known that the rest of Europe would have been astounded by the news of regicide – the killing of a king – and would be watching their next moves closely. They also must have known that, following the death of King Charles, the Scots would welcome his son Charles, thus providing a catalyst for future royalist uprising everywhere. Perhaps given the fact that Cromwell and the New Model Army had beaten the Scots on several occasions in recent times coupled with the amount of work needed to be done to get their new house in order, England's leaders do not seem unduly worried about external powers for the meantime.

However, all that said, I doubt the Council of State expected to find Ireland on their agenda quite so quickly. They would have known of a treaty that had been concluded in January at Kilkenny (when they would have been solely occupied with the trial and execution of Charles I) in which Ormonde had acted on behalf of Charles to unite with Irish Catholics. This had been followed up by an invitation for Charles's son, also Charles, to come to Ireland. Coupled with this, Prince Rupert, Charles's strongest and most capable supporter, was raising a naval threat. To all intents and purposes, Ireland was preparing for war against England's new regime.

On top of this external challenge there was another matter of internal affairs to be addressed: the Leveller Party. This was formed to protect the interests and well-being of the ordinary soldiers who had fought for Cromwell and the New Model Army. They felt disenfranchised and that they were being overlooked by the Officer Corps. This would have struck a chord with Cromwell who had always looked after his troops. To a certain extent, I can sympathise with him: many a politician will be familiar with the near-impossible task of listening and supporting all those who present a grievance. In fact, the higher one rises, the harder it becomes to continue to be present on international, national and local matters simultaneously. But I do think he overreached himself on the Ireland issue. It was a bridge too far. On 15 March 1649, it was announced that he was to be the commander in chief for the Irish Expedition. It is said he did not really want to do it, but felt he must. For me, this was a huge political error. The Levellers came out quickly in their condemnation, branding him, with the utmost contempt a 'New King' and even going so far as asking, 'Oh Cromwell whether art thou aspiring – was it towards a new regality?' (*England's New Chains Discovered*, 1649).

The Levellers were not alone: a splinter group called the Diggers, based in Wellingborough, were even more vociferous. They demanded 'free-the-land-for-the people', which in essence totally undermined both freehold and leasehold land and properties, neither of which were policy for Cromwell's government. Then there were people like the 'Northern Prophetess' who demanded: 'The poor commoners needed to be given their proper liberties.'

But Cromwell was a man of absolutes and, on 9 May 1649, he announces to Parliament that he has appointed himself the title of Governor General of Ireland and prepares to travel to Ireland to quash the Catholic uprising. Perhaps he is frustrated by the incessant bickering within the country; perhaps he feels he needs a decisive action to show his strength and power. But I am not an apologist for him. There is no doubt in my mind that Cromwell's decision to go to Ireland was a mistake. He clearly should have sent either Ireton or one of the other senior generals he trusted.

However, he did go and must have thought it was God's Will that this was the way to lead the new nation. He must have also recalled what had happened in 1641 with the Irish and the slaughter of the non-Catholics and, given the strength of his faith, he would not tolerate a repeat of this.

Cromwell left London on 11 July and reached Dublin on 15 August 1649. What followed was a bloody and brutal campaign with particularly vicious attacks at Drogheda and Wexford that have coloured Irish attitudes about Cromwell to this day. The rules of war in the 1650s were very different to today: an attacking force, having got an upper hand, could order defenders to surrender in return for a safe passage out. It appears that whoever was in charge of the defence at Drogheda was not prepared to surrender but fought on. Cromwell, with the battles of 1641 in mind, further fuelled by his own religious conviction, showed no mercy and ordered the complete annihilation of the enemy: 'I am persuaded that this is a righteous judgement of God upon these barbarous wretches' (Morrill, 2022). The same tactic, and result, happened at Wexford. The message got through and other Irish towns capitulated with much less bloodshed. This is not to negate Cromwell's savage ruthlessness. I cannot help but think of Shakespeare's Macbeth who moves from 'brave Macbeth' to 'that … butcher' when his fellow military officers describe his actions on the battlefield. I have travelled a great deal around the world and have witnessed the barbarous use of force between fighting factions within nations, specifically the Sri Lankan civil war. War is always 'a bloody business' in every sense and so I make no further comment.

Cromwell stays in Ireland for the rest of 1649. This is significant because, and I cannot emphasise this enough, the new constitution is still so young with so much work to be done. Cromwell is kept abreast of news from Westminster by letter, and in January 1650 receives instructions from the Speaker about the land settlement in Ireland. He must have felt frustrated at being the man on the ground but dictated to by Parliament hundreds of miles away, and a Parliament that he was so instrumental in setting up. In addition, there were now rumblings in Scotland that needed attention. Bearing in mind that no real campaigning could take place in winter, Cromwell, in my judgement, should have returned to Westminster himself and handed what was left to be done in Ireland to the capable hands of Ireton.

Cromwell finally returned to England at the beginning of June 1650. He must have been greeted by a veritable sea of issues to address both in Parliament and at home. However, within four weeks he was off on the campaign trail yet again, this time to Scotland. While he had been away fighting in Ireland, Scotland had taken Charles I's son, Charles II as their King and were calling for their own governance centred on their Presbyterian beliefs. The cry around the country was: 'Presbytery and King'.

Again, Cromwell did not want to go. I feel sure that he must have felt he had already missed out on enough of the decision-making in Westminster while away in Ireland so he tried to persuade Fairfax to be in charge but to no avail. Fairfax maintained that the planned offensive nature of the expedition was an obstacle to justice. So yet again Cromwell found himself given command of an army of about 25,000 men. At least the home media was supportive. One editor stated: '[I]f we take a view of his actions from first to last, I may proclaim him to be the only "Novus Princeps" that I ever met with in all the confines of history.'

Cromwell took command and crossed into Scotland on 22 July. His opponent was General Leslie who decided to deploy a cat-and-mouse tactic, trusting in the terrain that would be challenging for the English army, further exploiting their weakness due to sickness and hunger following their long march north. However, Leslie had not thought about Cromwell's creativity – or experience as a soldier – soon to be evident in the Battle of Dunbar. Being heavily outnumbered, Cromwell introduced the element of surprise and attacked in darkness, breaking through the opposition's line at 6.00 am, chanting Psalm 46. The psalm is a confident declaration of God's protection, full of military imagery, and would have given Cromwell great moral strength in an hour of need. The Scots were routed and the Battle of Dunbar remains one of Cromwell's defining military successes.

On 7 September Cromwell enters Edinburgh city but not the castle. There followed a series of small battles around and beyond Edinburgh, but the castle stands defiant. Progress was further hampered by Cromwell himself being taken ill. He is now fifty-two years old; by seventeenth-century standards, he is well past middle-age and a lifetime of physical exertion on the battlefield is taking its toll. There is no doubt that his ill-health delays the Scottish campaign with the net result being no decisive victory over Charles II and Scotland.

Perhaps a little surprisingly, or maybe in an attempt to break the stalemate of small skirmishes lost and won, the Scots, under the leadership of Leslie and Charles II, decide to march south into England in search of royalist supporters. There were alleged to be Scottish royalists in areas of Lancashire and Wales but the residual effect of the 1648 campaign that had created a deep distrust of all matters Scottish was underestimated. As a result, the royalist supporters proved to be elusive and not as great in numbers as Charles II had hoped. Nevertheless, the King ended up at Worcester on 22 August 1651.

Cromwell, the seasoned veteran, advanced more cautiously and did not reach Worcester until he had amassed an army of more than 28,000. The King's troops totalled approximately 13,000. The action broke on the auspicious date of 3 September. Cromwell had the King trapped from west to east. He himself entered the field of fighting with his own men on the east front. The royalists were pushed back into Worcester to face their death, although the King manages to escape and later turns up in Paris. But the hour belongs to Cromwell. Hurriedly, he writes a letter to Parliament to report the victory, describing the battle as 'A very Glorious Mercy' from the point of view of the Commonwealth. Later he added, 'The Dimensions of this mercy are above my thoughts. It is for aught I know a crowning mercy.' This clearly shows Cromwell's personal belief in Providence and that he believes he has been fighting a just and holy war. High words but no doubt Cromwell felt justified in using them as even though he would go on to direct military campaigns from afar, this would be recorded as his last involvement on the battlefield. Finally, after two long and bloody years focusing on military matters, he can now turn his attentions back to domestic affairs and the increasingly troubled Rump Parliament.

*

On his return to London, Cromwell is hailed a hero. How could he think otherwise following his entry into the capital with huge cheers, banners, cries and yells of adulation on a scale not seen before. He was captain-general of the army with a proven track record on the battlefield, a member of the Council of State and still the MP for Cambridge. He sits on a variety of committees covering key matters like trade and the settlement of peace. These positions do not come without their perks: a salary of £4,000 a year from Parliament and free use of Hampton Court. He must have been seen as a really strong thinking man who once decided on a strategy wished to see it executed with speed and dedication. However, as he would soon discover, there is a world of difference between leading an army with clear decision-making skills, which resulted in orders being followed, to managing a government where debate is not only accepted but encouraged! He may have been the most powerful official of the government, but he was powerless to insist that his proposals were automatically accepted. It is therefore little wonder that he turned to his faith and to God for guidance and confidence for he knew he faced, in his role as quasi-leader, a veritable bucketload of problems in all four nations: England, Wales, Scotland and Ireland.

Perhaps the most pressing problem Cromwell faced on his return to London was the organisation of Parliament. This was still made up of the remnants of The Long Parliament purged into a 'Rump' and originally elected more than a decade previously in 1640. The old House of Lords had been removed so that Parliament was a single unit, but within it there was a section to carry out some of the responsibilities of the former Lords. The obvious solution would have been dissolution and new elections, as happens today when a government loses a vote of No Confidence or decides it needs a better working majority, as Harold Wilson did in October 1974. But, at the time, the Rump had little interest in ending its own authority, no doubt mindful that systems were relatively new and needed nurture rather than further overhaul. In addition, following Ireton's death in Ireland, Cromwell was lacking a close confidante. All senior figures, such as Prime Ministers, work best when they have a close senior colleague with considerable experience with whom they can sit down to discuss key issues, so maybe Cromwell felt vulnerable at this time, unsure who he could trust.

The question of a new Parliament or 'the new representative' as some called it was not straightforward: should existing MPs automatically stand again? And how could they prevent the return of royalists, Presbyterians or other hostile interests? Some argued for elections by 'recruiter' (filling seats gradually), others for appointing qualified men directly. These issues were first formally debated on 17 September 1651, only days after Cromwell's return. A bill for a new representative followed in October, setting 3 November 1654 as the final date by which the Rump must dissolve. Cromwell's only consolation was being placed at the head of the list for the Council of State.

Cromwell's next initiative was to call a meeting under the auspices of Speaker Lenthall with certain active MPs and experienced army officers to discuss and debate the key issue of the Settlement of the Nation. The central debate was whether England should become a republic or whether it should maintain some sort of monarchy. Somehow the idea of a real Commonwealth had been overlooked despite Cromwell's earlier suggestion for it. All this debate came at considerable cost, in all senses of the word. The war had cost the country heavily – in manpower, in the trust of the people and in real monetary terms – and it felt like Cromwell and government were continually embroiled in one concern after another. The Puritans, of all people, who had always concerned themselves with the quality of the lives of ordinary people, had failed to make any real impact and all the while the Rump kept busying itself with the improvement of laws. It is of course a topic that continues to top the agenda today, but given the ever-growing list of very real concerns for the nation, improvement of laws, at this time, seemed unnecessarily bureaucratic.

By the summer of 1652 the relationship between the Rump and the army had reached rock bottom with the army calling for a dissolution of Parliament. Cromwell and other senior figures worried about how to keep the soldiers loyal. Those who had created the Commonwealth believed in a political contract based on popular consent, with a singlechamber Parliament and an executive Council of State. The Act of January 1649 had declared the House of Commons the supreme authority in the nation – a principle supported by influential thinkers such as Milton – but Cromwell increasingly doubted whether the Rump could ever meet the needs of the people whose liberties he believed he had fought to secure.

By the beginning of 1653 the problems of the new Parliament seemed insoluble, allied with the army's resistance following the cut in pay for home-based soldiers to fund, instead, the sailors engaged in the expensive Dutch War. The key stumbling block was the franchise of the new electorate. This manifested itself in Parliament debating every Wednesday throughout February and March but still failing to satisfy sceptical soldiers. Some progress was made with the decision to reduce the amount of capital a citizen needed in order to qualify to vote to £200. This was still a sizeable sum of money and continued to rule out a large percentage of the population coupled with the other rather strange rule that existing Rump Members should be automatically returned. The in-fighting became unbearable: the only thing anyone could agree on was that Parliament should be dissolved immediately. Cromwell, who was beginning to think like any leading practical politician, knew that if there was to be a dissolution then there must be some form of interim council to replace it but not one made up of the existing Rump. The resultant compromise was stated by Cromwell to be: 'we desired they would devolve the trust over to persons of honour and integrity that were well known, men well affected to religion and the interest of the nation'. The 'We' was understood to encompass representatives from all sides and therefore agreed.

However, despite Cromwell's best efforts to safeguard this new and fragile democracy, other members of the Rump Government's actions dealt him a cruel twist of fate. In April 1653, Cromwell receives news that approximately one hundred members of the Rump were meeting in the main chamber in Parliament and discussing the new Bill, which, crucially, would have extended their own term in office. He sees this as a gross betrayal of trust, not only by fellow MPs but also by men who never fought for their country as he had. It is recorded that he justified his subsequent actions: 'Thus, as we apprehended, would have been thrown away the liberties of the nation into the hands of those who had never fought for it.' Frustrated, upset, betrayed, he summons a party of soldiers and rushes to Whitehall. It is 11.15 am on 20 April 1653.

Cromwell bursts in, does not bow to the Speaker but strides to his usual seat where he sits in stoney silence. I can picture the scene as I have sat at the corner seat of the fourth row for the last twenty-eight years that I have been in the House of Lords – a different chamber but the layout would have been similar.

With anger rising within him, Cromwell sits sullenly until he can no longer contain himself. He gets up, ignoring whoever has the floor, starts to walk up and down the middle aisle, berating the House for furthering their own interests in debating the Bill. As his voice rises in a crescendo, contemporary reports tell that he yells: 'It is not fit that you should sit as a Parliament any longer. You have sat long enough unless you have done more good.' A back-bencher tries to restore order, visibly shocked by Cromwell's outburst and his colourful language, but Cromwell retaliates: 'I will put an end to your prating. You are no Parliament, I say you are no Parliament I will put an end to your sitting.' Then, across the Chamber to Thomas Harrison, he barks, 'Call them in' and about twenty-five soldiers from Cromwell's regiment enter the chamber, (Morrill, 2022).

But Cromwell isn't done. He strides over to where the mace is lying – that symbol of parliamentary authority – and asks: 'What shall we do with this bauble? – here, take it away.' Turning to the near hundred MPs, he announces: 'It is you that have forced me to do this for I have sought the Lord night and day that he would rather slay me than pit me upon the doing of this work.' He picks up the Act of Dissolution Bill and orders his soldiers to clear the Chamber. The Clerk of the House records, in his own handwriting:

'This Day his Excellency the Lord General dissolved
this Parliament:
Which was done without the consent of Parliament'

It was an extraordinary moment in history, which made the headlines immediately. Cromwell would have known it would, and would not have wanted it to be hidden. However, somewhat ironically for him, the Bill did include clauses based on a new electorate and had no Recruiter clause. But the deed had been done, and the result was, in effect, the dissolving of the long-serving Rump Parliament.

Of course, Cromwell's decision to use military intervention to shut down a sitting Parliament was a serious breach of privilege and it left a mark on his reputation that he never escaped – neither in his lifetime nor beyond. He had fought for parliamentary government, yet now found himself forced to break it. It was an impossible position: he wanted a nation governed by consent, but the Rump left him infuriated by its seeming paralysis. He was a man of action, frustrated by inaction. After years of fighting and military leadership, I think it is easy to understand his view that only the army could keep the country from drifting into chaos. But with the Rump gone, there was still a need for a minor deliberative body. The Army Council created a minor parliamentary body known as the Barebones Parliament. In essence the military now had control, and it named Oliver Cromwell as Lord Protector.

CHAPTER 9

The Protectorate

On 4 July 1653, just three short months after the dissolution of the Rump Parliament, Cromwell as the accepted leader opens its replacement: the Nominated Assembly. He delivers a two-hour oration in a hot and crowded council chamber in Whitehall. His opening words:

> Gentlemen, I suppose the summons that hath bin Instrument all to bring you hither. Gives you well to understand the occasion of your, being here; Howbeit I haveing somewt to impart to you, which is an Instrumt drawne up by the consent and advice of the principall Offices of the Army which is a little (as wee conceive) more significant than the letter of Summons … Wee have not thought it a misse, a little to mind you the series of Providences wherein the Lord hath appeared dispencing wonderful things to these are Nacions, from the beginning of our troubles to this verie day (Morrill, 2022).

Without any notes, he continues to give an in-depth summary of the turbulent events of the previous five years. While impressive, I am not surprised that he delivered his speech without any written prompts, as he was not simply recounting recorded events, but had lived and breathed them himself. I am also not surprised that he mentions his faith and his belief in Providence which has guided all his actions. After nearly two hours, he moves towards the climax with his characteristic clarity and conviction:

> I have only this to say further, that affairs of the nation laying on our hands ....did require noe interupcion and might well aske some tyme which the Comon wealth'... I have within a weeke sett upp a Councell of State to whome the managing of affaires is commited. (Morrill, 2022)

I find this both fascinating and revealing. Fascinating that he can set up a Council of State within a week – a feat that leaves my mind reeling at the work involved but also suggests some naivety. As I have said before, he is a military man who is used to giving orders in the clearest terms and expecting them to be executed. But his use of the inclusive 'our hands' does also illustrate his sense of shared communal purpose. This conflict between his instinct for singular leadership and his belief in shared responsibility is ever present and it continues right through to the end of the speech: 'things have bin thus ordered, that your affairs will go on till you see Cause to alter this Council they having no authority nor longer to sitt then but then until you shall take further order' (Society of Antiquaries, London).

He outlines the objective of the new Assembly. He gives a review of events from the outbreak of the Civil War right up to the Battle of Worcester. He reminds the assembled company of the extraordinary events of 1648 leading to the trial and execution of the King in 1649. He also advocates for the vital importance of education and reminds his audience of his own appointment, in 1650 while he was away in Scotland, as Chancellor of Oxford University. This is interesting as it is almost as if he is laying out his CV to further support his position. He explains the terms and role that the Nominated Assembly was to play, which was to do the work of governing. He stated it would last until 3 November 1654, at which time there would be a complete review of how it had performed.

However, the Nominated Assembly did not perform well and, despite Cromwell's best intentions, only lasted until December 1654 – just five months. This was mainly because of a clash between two polar opposites – religion and law – which proved to be incompatible where governance was concerned. Cromwell was bitterly disappointed. There had been some worthwhile achievements but nowhere near enough to justify the Assembly continuing. The radical reformers who pushed for sweeping changes in Church and state had gone too far for the moderates, unsettling ministries and alarming the more cautious members. In the end, the moderates forced a vote on whether the Assembly should continue and they won it decisively. On 12 December the Nominated Assembly brought itself to an end, leaving Cromwell as Lord General, to carry on the work of government with his officials. Looking back on the episode, Cromwell admitted it was a story of his own 'weakness and folly'. He had appointed the Assembly in good faith, but the experiment had proved imperfect and the situation far more complex than he had hoped.

Meanwhile, a close ally of Cromwell, Major-General John Lambert, anticipating the possible demise of the Assembly, had been working on an alternative structure of how England might be ruled using examples of systems successfully employed by the army. Much thinking and discussion took place in Lambert's inner circle which included Cromwell himself. Lambert had fought at battles including Dunbar and Worcester and, like Cromwell, was an experienced military man. Questions were asked and debated. Who would lead this new structure? Cromwell was the only choice. Could he be King? Cromwell was adamant that his title, or the title of any leader, should not have any connotations of royalty, so this was swiftly rejected. However, he was also extremely conscious that the title needed to be strong: to send a powerful message not only to the domestic nations and their peoples who needed clear leadership after the civil wars but also to foreign leaders who would be watching and waiting to identify any weakness that they could exploit. So, just a few short days after the dissolution of the Assembly, Lambert suggested the *Instrument of Government* with Cromwell as its leader.

Initially, Cromwell was cautious of the *Instrument of Government*. He must have been wary about starting another form of governance after the recent failures of others, and he could see that it was not entirely practical. However, he also truly felt that God would wish him to continue playing a key role and if the Instrument was to be the best vehicle to carry out that role, he must accept it. The *Instrument of Government* divided into two broad parts: the restrictions of office, which set moral and religious qualifications for those who would hold authority, and the regalities, which dealt with the practical arrangements of government. These included Cromwell and his family being settled in the old royal palace at Whitehall, his new title of His Highness the Lord Protector, and the provision that future Protectors would be elected rather than hereditary. Much of the document reflected the hard lessons of the previous few years, even though Cromwell himself had been an MP for more than twentyfive years.

While Lambert worked hard, and at pace, to draft the Instruments, there continued to be obvious tensions in Parliament between the various factions over the removal of the Court of Chancery, despite the Assembly's impressive record of passing thirty Acts on a range of social and economic issues. Finally, on 12 December, the vote was taken to dissolve the Assembly and recorded: 'Upon this day made in the House that the sitting of the Parliament as constituted, will not be for the good of the Commonwealth.' This allowed Lambert and Cromwell to quickly step forward and present the *Instrument of Government* on 16 December.

Cromwell had long been concerned about the Barebones Parliament, which had been, in his mind, hostile to the army, shown most clearly in its reluctance to support the monthly assessments needed to pay soldiers. This was at a time when military support remained vital to the stability of the country

– not only to suppress pockets of royalist resistance but also to protect prominent figures such as Cromwell himself. A turncoat, Captain Bushell, had even prepared to assassinate him. Although Bushell was caught and executed, Cromwell would have been acutely aware of his own vulnerability as he strove to implement change. Leadership at this level is often a lonely and stressful place, and Cromwell must have felt that. MajorGeneral John Lambert increasingly fulfilled a crucial need for both political and personal support. It was, in my opinion, a sensible pairing: Lambert did not enjoy the cut and thrust of parliamentary debate, preferring instead to shape policy and draft legislation, leaving the impassioned oratory to Cromwell.

Thinking and reflecting on Cromwell's position at this time brings back my own personal memories as a new, young and enthusiastic politician. Having been elected, against all the odds, in February 1974 as MP for Northampton South, by just 179 votes after three recounts in a seat not won by a Conservative for fifty years, I began to settle in as the new boy, learning not only the ways of Parliament but also the personal dynamics and relationships that shaped Westminster. It was soon apparent that the Prime Minister, Harold Wilson, was likely to call another election as he did not have a working majority. My prognosis proved correct and another general election was called in October with the polls in Harold Wilson's favour.

In the interim I used all the communication skills I had learned as a marketing and advertising executive in my commercial life over the previous fourteen years in the UK, India and Sri Lanka to persuade my constituents that I deserved another chance as their MP. The decisive strategy for me turned out to be the postal votes of electors who had voted for me in the February and had then moved away but crucially were still on the same electoral register. My excellent team managed to trace everyone who we knew from our previous canvassing in February. I then wrote a personal, handwritten letter to each of them asking for their vote again. Uniquely I think, we had a 100 per cent response, which just covered my new majority of 142 and allowed me to keep my seat.

On my return to Westminster, it was clear that Ted Heath would be standing down as Leader of the Opposition. As luck would have it, I had begun to get to know Airey Neave MP who I already respected for his military exploits. He asked me if I would be his unofficial parliamentary private secretary (PPS) (unpaid) as he was determined to find the new Leader of the Conservative Party. I accepted with alacrity, and I booked rooms for meetings, sent out his messages and was a really enthusiastic PA. Initially, he had chosen Edward du Cann MP, and we had managed to secure about 120 MPs to support Edward only for him to withdraw his candidature as he had recently re-married.

Airey and I sat down together and went back to the drawing board. A weekend was approaching and he asked me to book meeting room J3 for the following two Tuesdays, which I duly did. We met on the Monday, and he told me he thought he had found the right person to lead our party and that he would share it with me, and me alone, in the next forty-eight hours. The hours passed and we met again. He told me that his suggestion for leader of the Conservative Party was a Mrs Margaret Thatcher MP.

We had our special meeting in J3, attended by the 120 du Cann supporters. Airey introduced Margaret who spoke of her ambitions. A vote was taken and, all but a handful, supported Mrs Thatcher. The rest is history. Margaret Thatcher was elected Leader of the Opposition with Airey as her key advisor. I remained as Airey's PPS. In response to my work and loyalty, Airey asks me what junior ministerial position I would really like if we won the next general election. I said junior housing minister, as I had been chair of the Islington Borough Council Housing Committee. Airey says: 'wonderful, relax' – he knows Margaret will listen carefully. The election takes place on 4 May 1979. The Conservatives win and Mrs Thatcher becomes the UK's first female Prime Minister. However, there is no one to suggest Michael Morris MP should be junior housing minister. Just a few short weeks before, on 30 March, my dear friend Airey was a victim of a fatal *Irish Republican Army* (*IRA*) attack, blown up by a bomb placed under his car, in the House of Commons car park.

Those events in 1979 showed me that politics is built as much on personal loyalty as on policy and that the higher you rise, the more vulnerable you become. With that in mind, I can better appreciate why Cromwell valued Lambert's presence so deeply during the creation of the *Instrument of*

Government. It had been designed to give the Protectorate a firm constitutional foundation and to anchor it in clear legislation and was very much the product of Lambert's hand, but supporting Cromwell's vision. Thankfully, when it was proposed on 16 December 1653, in Westminster Hall, it was adopted. There were continued rumblings that Cromwell should be 'crowned' but this was unacceptable to him. He was offered, and accepted, the novel title of 'Lord Protector for Life'.

It is a fairly obvious assumption that Cromwell would have played a role in the selection of the founder members of the Protectorate. It would have been similar to a new Prime Minster picking his cabinet. After what he had been through with the dissolution of the monarchy and the civil war, it is not surprising that the new Parliament include senior members of the military but not the landed gentry who had been so powerful under the King. Afterall, in Cromwell's view, not only would they be considered 'royalist' it was unlikely that they would adhere to Puritan principles.

At last, there seemed to be a structure for governance that showed real potential as it had divided up responsibilities; legislative matters and executive powers were to be kept separate. Legislative matters would be discussed and debated by Parliament, but executive powers would rest with the Protector and his Council. For example, a decision to go to war could only happen if there was a majority voting for it. However, it seems nobody spelt out any necessary size of a majority. I find this interesting as it is uncannily like Prime

Minister Cameron's Referendum on Brexit where, in the end, the majority in favour was really quite small.

With his new role as the head of a totally reorganised government, Cromwell took a detailed interest in areas such as the liberty of conscience, national security and the elimination of heresy. He was now Lord Protector for Life, ruling over not just England and Wales but also Scotland and Ireland, guided by the newly written constitution. I have no doubt that Cromwell, in his heart of hearts, decided he would do his very best to perform his civil responsibility with the same due care he had taken over his military campaigns. He had also been an MP for more than twenty-five years, so he knew how Parliament worked. I find it interesting that in that switch from military leader to Parliamentary figure, he also had to change his mode of communication. All through his military life, he had written detailed letters, most often immediately after the action that acted as an important record. Now, with his new position and stable Parliament he switches back to being a speech maker, honing the art of rhetoric, persuading his fellow MPs to his way of thinking. He was a powerful speaker – still such an important quality and skill for our MPs and others in public office today. Of course, Cromwell had his unshakable faith in God to guide him, which coloured and impassioned both his speeches and his actions.

In this new set-up, one of the key challenges he faced was to understand where the boundaries lay between his leadership role as Lord Protector and the protectoral role of central government. He knew he had responsibility to the nation and, yes, that position certainly came with the same trappings the King had enjoyed, such as being able to reside in two palaces: at Hampton Court and Whitehall. He would also have been seen as head of state by foreign diplomats, too, and I suspect was required to perform the same duties as our Foreign Secretaries of today. He opened and closed parliamentary sessions and when it came to his re-inauguration in June 1657, the ceremony was not dissimilar to what occurs today: the wearing of fine robes and a procession of certain senior members of the Upper House with the King or Queen reading the opening statement to direct their Parliament in its next term.

However, as far as I can see Cromwell did not have vast, unfettered political power and did not run the state. We know he was appointed for life, but the boundaries had been set in the written constitution, thereby establishing a defined and powerful executive and a succession of Parliaments with full legislative powers. Perhaps the most important changes made by the 1657 revised constitution were that Cromwell commanded the county militias and trained bands as well as having the right to declare war or make peace. Given the events of the previous decade, coupled with his own active military service in a time of war, I see this as a cautionary and sensible step from an experienced leader and not the work of a dictator driven by lust for personal power.

Difficult times call for decisive leadership and looking back over the past nearly four centuries between Cromwell and the world today, those leadership qualities are hard to find. There are people of the moment, like Winston Churchill who was a phenomenal wartime leader with his powerful rhetoric and bullish personality, which have come to be seen as the very epitome of British bulldog spirit. His famous speeches and phrases, learned by schoolchildren today, 'we will fight them on the beaches', 'their finest hour' and 'the Few' motivated and inspired a nation through its darkest days of war. However, even he could not maintain the nation's support once the war was over. Contrastingly, Margaret Thatcher had a strong leadership in peacetime. Not a warm person, but one who did not shrink away from difficult decisions and I quote: 'If you set out to be liked, you will be prepared to compromise on anything at any time and would achieve nothing.'

Another important change – one that Cromwell may have initiated or certainly supported – was the reintroduction of a new 'Other House' alongside a revived Privy Council. Cromwell was to be consulted on appointments to these bodies, but he was given no power of veto. Likewise, when it came to the appointment of senior civil servants, he was entirely excluded from the process. Where the Protector *did* hold authority was in his ability to veto parliamentary bills and to dissolve Parliament, provided a minimum sitting period had been met. Considering this all happened nearly five centuries ago many of today's rules have similarities. Frankly it is not far off what happens today if a government has a big enough majority in the Commons, although, unlike Cromwell and his Council, it does not have to consult anybody.

It seems to me that Cromwell and those involved with the setting up and administration of this new Protectorate saw it as part of their bid to ensure its success to introduce more transparency in governance. There are order books that record the meetings of the council and MPs' attendance at meetings. So, as far as I can see, Cromwell stuck to the rules in his dealing with Parliament. He was quite clear that when Parliament was not sitting the Council was vital. I have read the details of these early days of the Protectorate, and it is clear to me that Cromwell took enormous care to ensure there were checks and balances and was particularly mindful that neither he nor any successor could be tempted to act unilaterally as the former King had done. However, even with this new approach, there remained a key issue: Parliament was not sitting, so under the Constitution Cromwell had to share power with the Council. I can find no evidence that he attempted to go behind the back of the council or even undermine it. Later, there would be a great row over exclusions from the second Protectorate Parliament, but Cromwell played no part in it at all; it was all the work of the Council.

So, with the administration in place, Cromwell is free, or at least freer, to pursue his interests in both national and international, or foreign, affairs. Ever since his early days as an MP he has taken an interest in the New World Pilgrims – those devout Puritans who set forth for the new world of the

Americas in search of a life free of religious persecution. Ever the shrewd businessman, with best practises and economies learned from his days as a land agent and tenant farmer, Cromwell takes a renewed interest in the Western design: a project largely driven by commercial ambition within the City of London, which hoped to tap into the wealth Spain was drawing from the West Indies. Given Cromwell's new position and his own latent curiosity about overseas expansion, it is not surprising that he wanted the matter debated properly in Parliament. He took time to meet the Diplomatic Corps to better understand the situations in foreign lands and he adhered closely to constitutional procedure in doing so.

However, domestic affairs kept tugging at him. His title of Protector, with all its religious connotations, would have carried significant weight with him personally and he saw it as his duty to look after all his people, just as he used to do with the soldiers in his regiments. He wanted to see a programme of spiritual, moral and social reform across the nation to meet God's will guided by 'healing and settling', themes so prominent in his opening speech to the first Protectorate.

For Cromwell, protection of his people meant the army. How else could Scotland and Ireland be controlled? As far as England and Wales were concerned the key to internal peace was the army's presence. This would be the main area of policy on which Cromwell had to manage his fledging Parliament. On a personal level, which he felt was supported by God, was his belief in the need for a large army and yet the majority of his Parliament wanted to reduce its size. It was this point that was the catalyst for the dissolution of the first Protectorate in January 1655. I cannot help feeling a little disappointed in Cromwell on this decision. He had worked so hard and achieved so much; to my mind it belies a man who was feeling frustrated by bureaucracy, even if he had been instrumental in its creation. He was also aged fifty-six, considered almost old age at this time, and put simply, he must have felt exhausted. Parliament would not be replaced for twenty months, until September 1656, during which time a number of significant events took place.

*

Indeed, perhaps because of the dissolution of yet another government, uprising followed soon after, notably in the spring of 1655 by royalists and Levellers in the West Country at Penruddock. This proved that all was not quiet and stable in the country albeit it was dealt with promptly and successfully by the army. It had the immediate effect of making the government jumpy, worried and concerned that the traditional system of Lord Lieutenants was not equipped to manage a nation trying to return to peace and normality while still watching for pockets of rebellion and other 'miscontents'.

Lambert, his team and Cromwell must have discussed the way forward. Their answer was the creation of the majorgenerals to control ten (later becoming eleven) key parts of England and Wales, each fully equipped and, by August 1655, in full charge of the 'horse militia'. The men appointed were almost always former experienced military officers from Parliament's New Model Army. Their prime objective was to build a structure as a reserve for any emergency, particularly any further royalist insurrection. However, the system was costly, so each majorgeneral had the right to demand payment of a new tax called 'Decimation', namely 10 per cent of the income of all known royalists.

Cromwell supported the majorgenerals regional structure but was concerned about its effect on ordinary people trying to recover a normal life after the chaos of a devastating civil war. He worried in particular that it would undermine parts of his own Act of Oblivion passed in February 1652 and geared to normality. He was also anxious that there would be no consistency of control over ale houses, horse racing and even cock fights. In short, there had been a multitude of important domestic matters to be addressed even without a sitting Parliament.

On top of this, matters overseas were disheartening, with the complete failure of the Hispaniola expedition. This was the product of the Western Design to reduce Spanish dominance in the Caribbean (and have a share of the wealth coming out of it). The Hispaniola expedition had set Haiti in its sights but was a complete disaster. In a bizarre twist of fate, and by complete accident, the surviving members of the expedition were able to occupy Jamaica, thereby claiming it for England and Cromwell. Nevertheless, Cromwell took it hard, thinking God had turned against his actions.

I like to think that Cromwell, the Puritan, was reflective and even personally humbled by the defeat overseas. The failure of the Western Design – especially the disaster at Hispaniola – must have weighed heavily on him. Perhaps it sharpened his sense that God's purposes were not always clear and that harshness in matters of faith could be a dangerous thing. Whatever the cause, Cromwell's religious tolerance at home stood in striking contrast to his hatred of Catholicism abroad, particularly his deep hostility to Spain. At home he allowed English people to practise whatever faith they wished, provided their worship was 'quiet and peaceful'. It was under his leadership that the initiative to readmit the Jews into England was taken – a remarkable step for the age, and one that suggests a Protector increasingly aware of the need for compassion in domestic religious life.

On 17 September 1656, Cromwell opened his Second Protectorate Parliament with an even longer speech of three hours. The core of it was a determined defence of the Anglo-Spanish war, which had grown directly out of the failed Hispaniola expedition. He attacked the Spanish as the natural enemies of England and denounced the Fifth Monarchists at home as closet royalists. Two words summed up his strategy: 'security' and 'reformation'. He was particularly hot on 'disorder', which for him meant cracking down on activities such as cockfighting and horseracing – the very things the majorgenerals had been trying to regulate.

The first session of second Protectorate Parliament appeared to go well, and it ran until June 1657. I am convinced Cromwell, in principle, did not want to interfere. He was interested in constitutional revision, particularly because it would rest on people sent to Parliament by the people, as it is broadly today. This above all proves to me that Cromwell in his last days was a true Democratic politician.

There was to be one other major development. Cromwell believed the Naylor case (of alleged blasphemy) had highlighted the need not to bestow all legislative power. Cromwell and others thought that restoring a second chamber would provide greater safeguards with each house acting as a check on the other.

This is not quite how we operate today. After a Bill has been passed by the Commons it has to come to the Lords who may decide to make amendments, either by re-instating amendments rejected in the Commons or by passing new ones. Then, the Bill in its amended form goes back to the Commons who may decide to accept the Bill as amended by the Lords or reject some or all of the amendments. If they accept the Bill in its amended form it can become an Act. However, if the Commons insist on the Bill in its original form then it must go back to the Lords to think again. This can happen twice more but at the third time the Lords must give way, recognising that the Commons are the House elected by the people but the Lords are only appointed. What Cromwell initiated was a major step forward towards this form of democracy. He went further, stating that the new constitution met 'the two greatest concernments that God has in this world namely religion and civil liberty' (Cromwell, recorded in Morrill, 2022).

Surprisingly there were further attempts to offer the Crown to Cromwell but on 8 May 1657 he refused. He did accept a change that gave him the right to nominate his successor, which, in my view is sad, as it contravenes his work for true democracy whereby all leaders are elected. There has been much speculation as to why Cromwell refused the Crown and title of King, but I believe his own justifications are the best explanation. In his key speech of 13 April he stated: 'It would be far better to drop the title [of King] which good men so much opposed thereby compiling, indulging and being patient unto the weaknesses and infirmities of men who have been faithful all along in this cause…' (Morrill, 2022).

The title of Lord Protector was understood by ordinary people – the ordinary people that any government should and would serve. It was also a title that had been used for three years; at this time, this was a relatively long time of reasonable stability.

The Second Protectorate Parliament opened on 20 January 1658 and set to work on selecting founder members for the new Second House. Sadly, MPs were not impressed and started attacking the system, resulting in Cromwell dissolving Parliament again on 4 February.

In the months that followed, Cromwell continued his work and made three speeches covering issues such as the great dangers that faced the nation, at home and abroad, particularly from Spain, Catholics and royalists. The hostility of the Commons came from a combination of those who had been excluded from the first session but whose rights were upheld for the second and the elevation of many progressive proregime MPs. These speeches are markedly different from earlier ones because of their length: they are much shorter and hint at Cromwell's advancing age and impending decline into poor health.

But still he continues to work. He insists on taking an active role in restoring unity and loyalty in the army and, following the debacle of the Hispaniola campaign, focuses on the organisation of the City of London, including the positions of the lord mayor, aldermen and councillors. Perhaps this is a last-ditch attempt to put his house, the house that is the kingdom of England, in order.

By the summer of 1658 he was no longer himself and could not drive affairs forward as he once had. On 3 September 1658 – the anniversary of Dunbar and Worcester, dates he had always regarded as providential – Cromwell died.

*

The day before, 2 September 1658, four or five key friendly colleagues were gathered around the dying man trying to get him to name his successor. He does so in a failing voice and declares his son Richard to be his successor. Richard was no Oliver Cromwell. Indeed, they could not be more different as Richard was heavily in debt from the extravagant life he lived.

Following Cromwell's funeral, Richard is recognised as head of state for the next few months while various factions jockeyed for position. Richard himself decided to have the army as his protection rather than the Members of the Long Parliament. However, in this period of interregnum other forces are at work, namely General Monk and his team of loyalist Lords who are totally dedicated to the return of a monarchy in the form of Charles II. Conversely, the army are against the royalists and work through Parliament.

Initially, Richard as Lord Protector calls the third Protectorate Parliament to assemble on 27 January 1659 but he soon finds the parliamentarians hard to handle and, on 17 April, less than three months later, they convince him to dissolve the Council of Officers. Not surprisingly the Army Officers (his protectors) respond by persuading the Lord Protector to dissolve the third Parliament on 22 April. This then causes a reaction from the Council of Junior Officers who, on 26 April, petition for the return of the Long Parliament and at the same time other petitions pour in for the re-establishment of the Commonwealth.

The Council of Officers take the initiative on 7 May and force Richard to re-instate the Rump Parliament. This is followed on 19 May by Parliament electing a new Council of State. I can understand that Richard finds all these political manoeuvres more than he can cope with not least with the burden of debt still hovering over him. We do not know who Richard consulted but on 24 May 1659 he resigns as Lord Protector. Richard clearly felt a persecuted man and decided he had to leave England together with this family, which they did in early summer 1659 under the assumed name of John Clarke.

General Monk's campaign came to fruition when on 29 May 1660 King Charles II returned on his thirtieth birthday. Ironically for me personally he arrived in the famous ship *Naseby* sadly soon to be renamed *Royal Charles*.

CHAPTER 10

The House of Lords, 1642 to the Present Day

While conducting my research, I was struck by the interesting fact that every major change to the House of Lords has occurred during the reign of a monarch called Charles. The year 1649 saw the abolition of the House of Lords immediately after the execution of Charles I; the House of Lords returned at the reinstatement of a monarchy under Charles II; and, at the time of writing, Charles III is presiding over the removal of Hereditary Lords from the Upper House, something that, as a life peer, I support. Cromwell did not believe in hereditary positions of power either. Looking over some of the key moments in the colourful history of the House of Lords will demonstrate this.

The House of Lords was already well-established by the seventeenth century, but it was in 1621, just seven years before Cromwell was first elected to Parliament, that the first ever Standing Orders for the House were tabled. They consisted of thirty-three numbered clauses amounting to about 2,000 words and covered a range of topics from the constitutional to the practical: from the role of the Speaker to seating arrangements and fines for latecomers. The reason that these rules had to be set down on paper – or parchment as is actually the case – was that, at that time, the House contained such a high number of inexperienced members – 42 per cent – who needed to be instructed in how Parliament worked. In contrast, the Lower House (the Commons) was a larger body with a larger number of experienced members. This was the House that Cromwell joined when he was first elected as an MP for Huntingdon. I am sure he would have appreciated having a rulebook such as *Erskine May's Parliamentary Practice* – first published in 1832 with the latest edition being the twenty-fifth and published in 2019. (Incidentally, Erskine May was a pupil of Bedford School, as was I.) But as there was no such document for Cromwell, he was forced to learn 'on the job' so to speak and was, in my opinion, the better politician for it.

New clauses were added to the House of Lords Standing Orders in 1624 and in 1626 it was agreed that the rules should be read out at the beginning of every session. To my mind, this reveals a certain weakness: members of the Lords needed the rules explained, while in the elected Commons members simply learned the business by doing it. The Standing Orders continue to lie in the Parliamentary Archives today.

However, even if the House of Lords was home to a large number of inexperienced members when Cromwell was first elected as MP for Huntingdon in 1628, the House of Commons was not exactly a chamber of strength either – not least because the reigning monarch ultimately controlled politics. This is not to say there was no interaction between the Commons and Lords. Yes, there were divisions but there was also work going on steadily led by strong politicians from either House so that relations were bicameral as they are today. But for all the good intentions for collaboration, Parliament had to be summoned by a monarch and Charles I only summoned it when he was short of money. Charles was also complacent. The Lords comprised a mixture of those appointed by Charles himself and those he had inherited from his predecessors, but essentially, they were all still 'royalists'. Together these totalled 128, which, when added to the number of Bishops who also served, meant the House had a majority of about two-thirds, all of whom were indebted to the Crown for their appointment.

However, if the King was complacent, so were a number of his Lords, and many did not turn up for key votes, the results of which was a slow reduction in both the power and the influence of the Crown. In early 1641, the Opposition initially comprised about thirty members and was led by the Earl of Bedford, a very effective operator, who built up loyalty to the parliamentary cause by engaging his fellow members and encouraging them to turn up and vote on important matters of state. The King responded by making seven of his Peers Privy Councillors in a bid to shore up support for himself. Somewhat ironically, all seven were well-known for their leaning to the idea of a Commonwealth but perhaps this says more about Charles's lack of understanding of his Lords than a real threat of constitutional change at this point. Sadly, the Earl of Bedford died in May 1641. I say sadly as, with his demise, the possibility of really meaningful dialogue between King and his Parliament is further reduced. The King had also planned to give office to some of the popular leaders in the Commons like Pym and Holes but for reasons unknown this did not happen. However, the two Houses did work together on some constitutional Bills like the Triennial Bill, which was passed by the Lords on 5 February 1641 and ensured that there would be an election of a Parliament every third year whether the King summoned it or not. As previously mentioned, Cromwell had spoken in the Commons suggesting Parliament should be summoned every year but colleagues persuaded him it was not practical.

At the same time, the ongoing case of Thomas Wentworth, Earl of Strafford, provided a decisive moment in the struggle between Crown and Parliament. Strafford was a key advisor to King Charles and had served as a ruler in Ireland with notable severity. Charges had been brought against him that, while in Ireland, he had been levying money by force and imposing an oath upon the subjects there. He was also suspected of wanting to use the Irish army to enforce obedience in England and support a Crown ruler. The Commons took up the cause against him, whereas the Lords, who were sensitive about their judicial responsibilities, felt it was for them to decide a case of high treason that this was alleged to be. There followed row after row: Commons and Lords locked in a stalemate about which House should preside over such a serious charge. In the end a deal was done by Pym and Hampden based on a change of procedure, allowing arguments to be stated on both sides. When the legal case against Strafford begins to break down, the Commons found a way through by introducing a Bill of

Attainder, which allowed Parliament to declare him guilty without a formal judicial verdict. On 21 April, the Commons pass the Bill, 204 votes to 59, and passed it to the Lords to debate. Pressure was mounting on the Lords to approve the Bill, especially as the people of England were now exercising their right to protest and had come to Westminster in their thousands, brandishing weapons, calling out for justice and demanding Strafford's execution. The Lords continued to debate the case for a week. On the eighth morning, the Attainder Bill passed, both Houses petitioned the King to find Strafford guilty. Charles complies with their demands and the net result was Strafford was executed on Tower Hill on 10 May 1641. This marked a defining shift in power away from the Crown while simultaneously lessening the authority of the Lords, too.

It seems to me that in the months that followed there was a continual three-way power struggle between the Crown and the two Houses of Parliament. The King tried to bolster his numbers in the Lords with the appointment of some new members who had to pay for their title. Perhaps not much has changed as, since I have been in the Lords, I suspect financial donations may have been made to one or other political party, only for the donor to then appear in the Lords.

In quick response to Charles's appointment of Lords, the Commons focused on the exclusion of Bishops and catholic peers in the Upper House with the introduction of the Root and Branch Bill, which essentially called for the abolition of episcopacy. It was read twice by the Commons on 27 May, but the Lords threw it out on 8 June 1641.

Next, the Commons set its sights on depriving Catholic peers of their votes but in the succeeding weeks, despite their being much interchange between the two Houses, no decision could be reached. Almost in exhaustion the Commons then decide to appeal to the nation by drawing up and publishing the Grand Remonstrance. This, as has been explained earlier, was a manifesto of an indictment against the King for his mismanagement of the country along with a catalogue of reforms people wanted endorsed by the MPs. Interestingly, the Grand Remonstrance did not get passed to the Lords as, Pym pointed out, many of the complaints it sought to address were, in effect, caused by Lords. It was passed by the Commons on 22 November. But, just a few days later, the King returned from Scotland confident he had the Scots on his side, which gave him renewed confidence in his own power as well as in his appointed Lords.

This tit-for-tat, continual yo-yoing and jockeying for power was to become the lasting hallmark of a constitution that was begging for a complete overhaul. The struggle over Strafford's fate showed just how far the old system had drifted: a King intervening, two Houses pulling in opposite directions and a public inflamed to the point of becoming a menace. It would take more of this to-ing and fro-ing, more allegiances and defections, before definitive actions could take place – not to mention a civil war and, ultimately, the abolition of a monarchy. But the Strafford affair marked the moment when the balance began to tilt decisively away from autocratic royal rule and towards a Parliament determined to assert its authority.

What followed was a never-ending series of complex crises that pushed Parliament and Crown further apart and steadily weakened the old constitutional order. Pym kept up the pressure, probing the Lords' delays and obstructions, but events in Ireland and the King's meddling, from the Impressment Bill to the disastrous appointment of Lunsford as the Lieutenant of the Tower, meant that Parliament just could not focus on itself to bring about sensible, considered reform. In the midst of the fervent atmosphere, Westminster was besieged by crowds of demonstrators, siding with the Commons, calling for 'No bishops' and 'no popish Lords'. The King, feeling the pressure, quickly dumped Lunsford and replaced him with Sir John Byron, but I suspect this was viewed as nothing more than a token gesture by the swarming crowds who stayed at Westminster and continued to protest, with swords drawn. In my fifty plus years in Parliament, I have witnessed many a heated debate, several that have divided a whole nation, not only Westminster, such as Brexit, but nothing comes close to the violence of feeling – or action – across England in the 1640s. The Lords, feeling threatened, applied to the King for a guard, while the Commons refused to join them. When the bishops claimed they had been kept out of Parliament by violence and declared recent proceedings void, the Commons impeached twelve of them for treason. They were in prison by nightfall.

The King, unable to resist interfering, tried to impeach six Members of the Lords and arrest MPs, only heightening the tension. Pym then exposed the Lords' own daily journal recording like a modern Hansard and used it cleverly to catalogue and present the obstructions and delays the Upper House had thrown in their path. Matters worsened when peers discovered the King was plotting to recruit foreign troops into England. For a brief moment the two Houses united to demand control of the militia, but the King fled to York, leaving many of his supporters in the Lords disillusioned and drifting away. By April 1642, eightytwo were absent, and when the King then demanded his supporters join him in York, a mere thirty-two responded to his call. The others chose to obey Parliament and stayed in Westminster. As Thomas Hobbes later perceptively observed, 'it was a strange thing that the whole House of Lords should not perceive that the ruin of the King's power and the weakening of it would be his ruin and the weakening of themselves'. This captures perfectly how blind the Lords were to the consequences of undermining the very authority that sustained them, the results of which would spell the beginning of the end of the then House of Lords.

*

Returning to my protagonist, Oliver Cromwell. He was certainly not a silent by-stander throughout this time. As previously reported, he made a record number of speeches in 1641 and 1642 and closer examination reveals that there were three that were particularly relevant to the topic of governance. On 12 August 1641, he called for thirteen bishops to be expelled from the Lords; on 29 October 1641, he spoke again about the controversial appointment of Bishops to the Lords and on 10 December 1641, he spoke about the interference of peers in by-elections. Not long after this, he is called away to the field of battle and does not return to being an active politician until the summer of 1646, but these records clearly show his views. I would maintain that rather than seeking a full abolition of the Lords, Cromwell wanted them to stay but to stay fairly and not abuse their position of power.

Throughout the Civil War, both appointed Lords and elected MPs took active roles on both sides although somewhat ironically, the military leaders, certainly in the early stages of the conflict, were all from the House of Lords. The King had Lords Strange and Herbert under his command, together with the Earl of Newcastle whereas prominent figures such as the Earl of Manchester, Lords Brooke and Essex, sided with Parliament. Perhaps not surprisingly there were twice as many peers on the King's side as opposed to those on the side of Parliament. The King's Council ran the King's operations but people such as Prince Rupert did all they could to diminish the authority of the Council.

The big question was whether the King would compromise and allow more power to his government, but it was known he had an aversion to this notion. He was repeatedly presented with propositions restraining peers from sitting or voting in Parliament without the consent of both Houses, and at Uxbridge he was again asked to pass a Bill to that effect. The net result was bleak all round: if the King won, he had little time for Parliament; if Parliament won, peers who sided with the King would be excluded. Only about thirty peers were still attending and even they knew the role of the Upper House would be diminished. After this secession the Upper House was weakened in its relationship with the Lower House. The first real test came when the Commons applied to the Scots for armed assistance against the King; they consented and passed the Solemn League and Covenant on 20 September 1643, establishing Presbyterianism in England and Scotland. Leadership then recognised the need for a coordinated body and out came the Committee of Safety, even though arguments went back and forth until it was finally signed on 16 February 1644. Unfortunately, by the end of 1644 most of the parliamentary peers had been discredited in the field. To make matters worse for them, an Ordinance of 30 August 1646 declared all titles conferred since 20 May 1642 null and void, a stark reminder that unless compromise could be found, there might not even be a House of Lords regardless of who won.

Cromwell, ever the tactician, capitalises on this wave of antiLords' sentiment and proposes that there should be a clean sweep in governance with the installation of new blood, choosing those who have a proven trackrecord of leadership. Naturally, there was the inevitable friction between the two Houses, but the end result was the formation of the New Model Army, a fighting force of some 22,000 men with Sir Thomas Fairfax named as its first Commander. In Westminster there was a complete revolution in relations between the two Houses, at least for the duration of the Civil War. The relative strengths had also changed, with the Commons from August

1645 restarting recruiters for vacant seats, and by the end of 1646 their numbers had increased by 235. This infusion of new blood helped make the Commons more representative, while the Lords had become less representative and numerically weaker, with average attendances of under twenty.

Not only was there a shift in power between the two Houses but also another power struggle between King and Parliament. Momentum was gathering in wider society as army congregations, young men and citizens of London began to voice democratic ideas with a freedom made possible only because the Civil War had loosened old restraints. The voice of the people was not only loud and clear but also amplified due to the recent surge in printing and pamphleteers who were able to present their ideas in written form and reach larger audiences. One such writer was Lieutenant Colonel Lilburne who challenged the power of the House of Lords. He was summoned by the Lords, found guilty and sent to Newgate prison. When he appealed to the Commons they were in no mood to interfere or create a quarrel, but this would be damaging. More pamphlets appeared. Overton published *An Alarm to the House of Lords against their insolent usurpation of the common liberties and rights of this nation*; he too is removed to Newgate.

A deluge of both pamphlets and anger followed. Claims were made that the Lords were undermining the Commons, that Titles were awarded simply to help the King, and people began to ask who gave the Lords power to oppress and obstruct. Pamphleteers declared that 'our present House of

Peers are no legal judicature; away with pretended power' (Overton, 1646) and the cry went out: 'O all ye freemen or commoners of England… petition to your own House of Commons… to desire them speedily remove them before the kingdom be destroyed' (Lilburne, 1649). In London there was widespread sympathy for Lilburne but this still did not move the Commons. However, the new chaplain to the Model Army found sectaries, officers and men alike, 'vehement against the King and against all government' (Edwards, 1646). By not officially coming out against the Lords, the Commons were now in danger of being tarred with the same anti-government brush. I think back to my days of running the Conservative Party campaign in the London Borough of Islington in 1968 where we did not have a single councillor. The feeling was definitely anti-government, not just anti the-current-ruling-government. However, after deploying a mass leafleting campaign, highlighting the failure of the then current Labour council, we won forty-seven seats out of sixty. It was important to engage with the disenfranchised – those who blamed 'government' for all problems and to offer them a real alternative to the existing party in power.

On 26 July petitions were presented from the Common Council and when both Houses returned negative answers a mob rushed to Westminster, tackling first the Lords and then the Commons. The army, stationed nearby, declared its intention to maintain the independence of Parliament and worked with it to keep the show on the road. The House of Lords, however, was deeply affected. Their numbers were greatly reduced as nine had joined the army and eight had ceased to attend and although there was some rapport between army and Lords, the real stumbling block was the army's continued frustration at the seeming lack of any reduction of the power of the Lords. Ireton's *Heads of the Proposals of the Army* of 1 August 1647 made this clear. Lilburne, who had once called Cromwell 'the greatest antiLord in England', now accused him of becoming a 'patron, approver, and protector of them in all their arbitrary, illegal and tyrannical usurpations'. (Lilburne, 1649). One can only imagine how infuriating this accusation must have been to Cromwell, a feeling I shared when I started my campaign to win Islington Council in 1968.

Meanwhile, Charles had accepted nothing. Rankandfile soldiers were growing impatient and dissatisfied. As a result, they produced *The Case of the Army truly stated* and *An Agreement of the People*, both offered to the free Commons of England. Cromwell and Ireton were blamed for inaction, but Cromwell defended his position by admitting that he concurred with the agitators that sovereignty should be recognised as residing in the people and the people's representatives. In the end, Cromwell carried the day to set up a committee deploying his impassioned oratory skills:

> We all speak to the same end, and the mistakes are
> only in the way. The end is to deliver this nation
> from oppression and slavery, to accomplish that
> work that God hath caried us on in, to establish our
> hopes of justice and righteousness in it. We agree

thus far, I think we may go thus far further, that we all apprehend danger from the person of the King and from the Lords. All that have spoke have agreed in this too. (Morrill, 2022)

The Council sided with Cromwell and Ireton and, although much discussion came forth, the conclusion was clear: the supremacy of the House of Commons was declared, even though neither legislative nor judicial rights of the Lords were abolished.

But, as we all know, politics can change suddenly. The Levellers now announced that the King should be brought to justice and the House of Lords should be totally abolished. Then came the dramatic news that the King had fled Hampton Court to the Isle of Wight. When Charles asked to come to London, the Lords wanted him to accept four propositions but the Commons, emboldened by their recent successes, insisted he must accept them outright. Charles refuses and so, on 3 January 1648, the Commons votes to make no more addresses to the King, a move the army immediately supports. The Lords hesitate, but when regiments appeared in Whitehall, their opposition collapses and sixteen Lords agreed to the Commons' resolution on 15 January.

Although both Houses briefly adopted the army's policy, calm quickly evaporated. The Levellers demanded that the Lords should merge with the Commons in one House, while William Prynne flooded the market with pamphlets defending independent peerage, failing to see that by early

1648 independent peerage had ceased to apply to the existing House of Lords. On 28 April 1648, with civil war looming again, the Commons voted, by 65 to 99, not to alter 'the fundamental government of the kingdom by King, Lords, and Commons', and on 6 May both Houses concurred, but unity soon broke down. The Commons insisted the King *must* accept three propositions, including Presbyterianism for three years and Parliamentary control of the military for ten years. Once again the Lords disagreed, but, perhaps knowing that their power was continually eroding, they eventually yielded.

The Isle of Wight Treaty (18 September–27 November 1648) satisfied both the Lords and much of the Commons but outside Parliament Levellers and army officers condemned any settlement preserving the monarchy and the Lords. Their protests shaped the Remonstrance of 20 November, asserting that supreme power must lie in the people's representatives 'without appeal to any created standing power', a direct challenge to the Lords. Cromwell dismissed the Treaty as 'this hypocritical agreement', illustrating quite clearly to me that he did believe in proper protocols and procedure. Remember, too, that he was away in Scotland at the time of these debates, not returning to Westminster until after the Commons' vote of 4 December and the ensuing Pride's Purge. While attentions undoubtedly turned to the King's trial, the Lords found themselves increasingly irrelevant and scratching around to find any role in the settlement of the kingdom.

The events of January 1649 are well known: Charles I is brought to trial, found guilty and executed. England is no longer a monarchy but instead ruled by the army with Oliver Cromwell as leader. Two Houses of government remain but the future of the Lords hangs in the balance. Recent living history has seen it too closely aligned to the ruling monarch and, with the monarchy now abolished, there is a feverish atmosphere to finish what has been started and see the end of the House of Lords, too. However, the mood among the conservative section of the Commons, including Cromwell, was to keep the House of Lords. Although impassioned and full of conviction, Cromwell is also a man who believes in checks and balances and wants to keep the House of Lords to help hold the House of Commons to account. But, as is the very nature of democratic politics, votes can go either way and in February 1649 a motion to abolish the House of Lords is presented: 'That the House of Peers in Parliament is useless and dangerous and ought to be abolished'. The motion is carried 44 to 29. The nub of the issue was summed up succinctly by one Member: 'It may be asked, by what law the House of Lords could be laid aside by the Commons. Answer: by the same law which is the supreme law: the general good' (*England and Wales. Parliament*, 1649).

The postexecution government was necessarily interim, shaped by Pride's Purge and the Rump, with large areas of the country remaining unrepresented. Former Lords reacted variously: some stood for election, others hesitated, but Cromwell, ever the awake politician, convened a conference that produced a new engagement. By October 1649, Members were required to promise faithfulness to the Commonwealth without a King or House of Lords, and, after 20 April 1650, anyone refusing the oath lost access to the courts. Increasingly, former peers accepted a republican form of government. I find it encouraging that among the first to sign up to take their oath and pledge allegiance to the Commonwealth were the Earls of Northampton and Bedford. Perhaps not so surprising as both counties were and to a point still are counties with a tradition of religious non-conformity, but, nonetheless, proof of sensible, democratic leadership in the East Midlands!

The Commonwealth struck the Lords who refused to comply both politically and socially: they were deprived of their privileges, given no immunity from arrest and stripped of their titles. Royalist peers faced heavy fines, often ruinous, especially for those who had raised funds for the King. With the economy weakened after war, the old aristocracy suffered deeply. Meanwhile the army was in the driving seat, and Cromwell worked closely with them in uncharted constitutional territory, with one Assembly wielding nearunlimited powers.

As Cromwell wrestled with creating a stable political system, he moved from leader to Lord General, Protector, and finally Lord Protector for Life, guided by *The Instrument of Government* and *The Humble Petition and Advice*. He came to believe that a second chamber was necessary to arbitrate between Parliament and Protector. The army agreed, warning that without one there was a danger of recreating a new House of Lords and sliding back towards monarchy. Their warnings proved timely. In February 1657, *The Humble Address and Remonstrance* proposed a new upper chamber; Cromwell carried the day and sixtythree members were selected – mainly military men and experienced officials, with some former peers impressed by his reforms. Debate followed over whether to call it 'The House of Lords' or 'Other House', but Cromwell, unwilling to see wrangling, dissolved Parliament. He opened the Second Protectorate Parliament in January 1658, and I am sure he was intent on securing the return of a second chamber, but his death prevented him from seeing it through to fruition.

I have pondered on why Cromwell, only on his death bed, named his son Richard as his heir. He must have known that he was not the right man for the job. Richard was not a military man nor a politician, so his life-experience had given him no preparation for the role. The only defence I can think of is that Cromwell was taken ill so quickly that he did not have time to think of a suitable alternative. Given that the laws of primogeniture were prevalent in all society at the time – whereby the eldest son inherits all – I presume Cromwell, in his final hours, resorted to it as a known and commonly held belief. I maintain that he wished for a second house in Parliament but ran out of time to see it instigated. Perhaps by naming Richard as heir, he knew he would need to be supported in the role and that through that support, the second house would come to be. That said, I doubt Cromwell would have wanted to see it returned by a monarch. Charles II was briefed that the key to the future of the country lay with the elected House of Commons and the House of Lords appointed by the monarch alongside hereditary and existing appointees. As it happened, with the restoration of the monarchy, the Constitutional Rights of the House of Lords were undiminished.

The House of Lords today

The Labour government, elected 4 July 2024, promised to shake up the UK's unelected House of Lords. The Prime Minister vowed to transform the archaic Upper House by removing all hereditary peers and introducing a retirement age of eighty. Later, in 2025, due to resistance from both Labour and Liberals the reforms were quietly dropped. Personally, I feel strongly that all hereditary peers should go and numbers should be reduced to about fifty fewer than the number of elected MPs in the House of Commons.

But this was not new news. Ironically, almost a century previously, on 25 March 1925, a Conservative government debated a motion calling for the reform of the House of Lords and particularly for it to be reconstituted on a popular basis rather than a hereditary one. The other key element that was debated was the number of peers and it was suggested that they should total from 350 to 400.

However, at the time of writing, it now seems that 2026 will see the end of all hereditary peers, probably before the end of the summer. Later in the year there will be a debate on the report of the 'Committee on Retirement and Participation' set up in January 2026 and due to report to the House on 31 July 2026. I have given my evidence in writing, highlighting that, in my opinion, new life peers need to have considerable life experience which probably means they will be in their forties. Additionally, there should be no automatic appointment of previous MPs even those who have been Prime Minister. I am comfortable with what seems a consensus that all must retire by age eighty, providing they have been participating up to that point. This will reduce the membership to approximately 760, still considerably more than the 650 elected MPs in the House of Commons. I myself have told my leader, Lord True, that I do not, in our modern world, support the concept of hereditary succession so will abstain in all votes about hereditary peers. So, after a century of debate there will soon be no hereditary peers and King Charles III will reign with peers appointed to the House of Lords on merit.

The new Select Committee, charged with debating the future of the House of Lords, has created an important opportunity to look at all aspects of governance and our constitution. There are many lessons to be learned, and we can look to our past to be guided. However, for any changes to be really worthwhile and enduring they must also reflect our society today. The selection of future peers must be truly representative of the diversity found in the UK. It is interesting to note that Canada has just completed such an exercise in the selection of members for its Senate. By having a House of Peers that is more representative of our home nation it will also help to inform our involvement with the rest of the Commonwealth and our overseas territories.

The House of Lords must also consider the role of the royal family in Parliament and wider governance – perhaps starting by addressing the size of the current royal family 'employed' by the nation with the possibility of streamlining it, following the example of other royal households in Europe. In seems both prudent and appropriate to review the financial support that the royal household receives from the nation together with the sensitive subject of taxation.

There is also the question of religious representation in the House beyond the Church of England which would give peers the benefit of understanding other leading faiths, which are followed by millions of Britons around the country. Today, in Richmond House, we have a multi-faith prayer room for private prayers, but this is located at the far end of the parliamentary estate. We might consider, on nominated daily prayers, celebrating a special prayer from other faiths. As I have a close association with south and south-east Asia, particularly with Sri Lanka, home of multiple national faiths, I would welcome this.

I was reminded of this recently when I received a Christmas card from the president, council and staff at The Buddhist Society, signed on one side by the President of the society, Dr Desmond Buddulph CBE, with a particularly moving verse on the reverse, which reads:

Though one man conquers
A thousand times
A thousand men in battle.
He who conquers himself is
The greatest Warrior.

Dhammapada, 'Thousands' (verse 103)

I am not one to recommend secularism but if we are to remain a liberal, caring, pluralistic society, we need to find a way to blend our Constitution with our faiths. I am certain that Cromwell would have concurred with this message. For all his faults, Cromwell understood the importance of representation and fair regulation. He also knew that the balance of power was far from equal and in urgent need of reform. These are lessons we must keep firmly in mind today: for constitutional change to endure, it must be fair, genuinely representative and inclusive of the nation and the people that it serves.

CHAPTER 11

Reflections on Cromwell

On entering the Cromwell Museum in Huntingdon, housed in the grammar school that he himself attended as a young boy, visitors are greeted by a large portrait by Robert Walker. Measuring nearly two metres in height, the portrait is almost life-size and allows visitors the unique opportunity to consider Cromwell the man. Clothed in a shining metal breastplate worn over a yellow padded jacket, his boots adorned with spurs, Cromwell is dressed as a senior calvary officer and holds a wooden baton – the general's baton – representing his high rank and authority. His outward gaze engages his viewer with an intensity that is almost disarming. Behind him a highly stylised landscape with gunmetal-grey clouds symbolises the turbulent and stormy days of the Civil War.

Over the portrait is a sheet of glass, carefully placed to protect the painting, now nearly 400 years old. On the glass lies a collection of words and phrases that have all been used to describe Cromwell, from his public, official titles of Lord Protector and Parliamentarian to revealing observations about his character – devoted husband and father, music lover and practical joker. But for every positive quality or title there is another that contradicts and testifies to another, less favourable, view of him: dictator, war criminal, hypocrite.

On looking at the picture and the words, one is reminded that we are all a complex mix of both virtues and vices. We all have our follies and our faults. Who better to sum up the complexities of human nature than Shakespeare: 'The web of our life is of a mingled yarn, good and ill together.' Spoken by the First Lord in *All's Well that Ends Well*, rather aptly a nobleman and a soldier, the character shows us that we are shaped by the events of our lives. Cromwell is an infinitely colourful character; I believe his strong character was moulded by the extraordinary times in which he lived and the events that he was not only witness to but participant in. I consider it a huge privilege to have been able to research and write about a man I have long admired and, in doing so, the character I have found has only enhanced that admiration.

For me, his strength of character and his endless commitment to his country (of England, Wales, Scotland and even Ireland) was due to his devotion to God. It was his ardent faith that guided him in all his actions and provided him with a lifelong concern for the welfare of all his fellow men. Additionally, his tolerance in religious matters in a time of some upheaval has to be admired. He was more than aware of all the different sects of non-conformity swirling around the country, but remained comfortable in his own faith as a Puritan and belief in Divine Providence. So comfortable in fact that it was his own initiative to invite those of the Jewish faith to return to the United Kingdom.

His military prowess proved to be exceptional with numerous successes on the battlefield. It was his clear yet compassionate leadership that created a devotional response from all soldiers under him, regardless of their rank. His excellent horsemanship lent him the courage to lead bravely and decisively, conquering all who stood before him. In addition, he was a good communicator, never failing to send messages to Parliament reporting what had happened on the battlefield. Yet, throughout all his experiences of warfare, he never failed to acknowledge the part that God had played in his success: in his battle report to the Speaker of the House of Commons, Cromwell describes the great parliamentary victory at Naseby in June 1645 to be 'None other than the hand of God and to Him belongs the glory'. Some would claim he was ruthless but I could find no evidence. Instead, I found a man who was committed and totally focused on completing the project in hand.

Cromwell did not believe in royalty and thanks to him we have a Parliament unique in itself with no written Constitution but a House of Commons full of MPs elected by the people as he was in Huntingdon and later in Cambridge. It was his strength of will and determination that removed the 'Divine Right of Kings'. Yet, here we are, more than three hundred and fifty years later and still we have a residue of that belief in the everyday rhetoric of the Church of England. The current fourth paragraph of our daily prayer still begins: 'Almighty God, by whom alone Kings reign, and Princes decree Justice.' I baulk every time at the phrase 'Princes decree Justice'. They do not! This serves to remind us just how much Cromwell did achieve in overturning an establishment – the autocratic rule of Kings – that had existed for hundreds of years. He gave us a two-tier Parliament: the House of Commons and, on his death bed, the restoration of an embryonic House of Lords.

It was Cromwell's vision to launch the concept of the Commonwealth rather than the more fashionable Republics that were appearing over much of Europe at the time. The Commonwealth today consists of fifty-six independent countries across Africa, Asia, the Americas, Europe and the Pacific. Thirty-three of the world's smallest states are members of the Commonwealth, each with a population of 1.5 million or less, including three Crown Dependencies and fourteen Overseas Territories. A total of 2.7 billion people live in Commonwealth countries, of which 60 per cent are aged twenty-nine or under. These are startling statistics, and I ask myself would the creator of the Commonwealth be comfortable with the attention – or lack of – that the British government gives to it today? I do not think so. But as one who is a regular attendee at Prayers in the House of Lords before the start of work every day that Parliament sits, I think it is time to consider all the different faiths both in the United Kingdom and the wider Commonwealth. My hope is that it would lead the way to a more representative Upper House and through that, one that is more conscious and considerate of difference within the country and the wider Commonwealth, too.

As the words on the previously mentioned portrait testify, opinions on Cromwell have always been divided. In May

1654, poet John Milton, not a friend but a contemporary who respected Cromwell, wrote: 'If that man [Cromwell] than whom no one has been considered more just, more holy, more excellent, shall afterwards attack that liberty which he himself has defended, such an act must necessarily be dangerous and well-nigh fatal not only to liberty itself but also to the cause of all virtue and piety' (Milton, 1654).

He clearly admired Cromwell for all his virtues and ideals but was also aware of the potentially catastrophic damage he could do if he failed to uphold those virtues. I think the way the country and the British people have chosen to remember Cromwell over the centuries since his death reveal more fully just how complex his memory and his legacies really are. In short, nothing to do with Cromwell is ever straightforward, as my next example will demonstrate.

There is a statue of Oliver Cromwell that resides in Westminster, one that previously resided on Cromwell Green – a testament to his enduring legacy to democracy. The original plan was for the statue to be unveiled on 25 April 1899 to mark the three hundredth anniversary of Cromwell's birth. The idea had been then Prime Minister Gladstone's, back in 1894, and was then promoted by Lord Roseberry when he took over as Prime Minister later in the same year. (I am indebted to William Wallace for the fascinating details he has published.) When the Liberals lost power, it fell to Lord Salisbury to take over the project, which he duly did. However, when the anniversary finally arrived, the actual unveiling had to take place at 7:30 in the morning, to avoid demonstrators, such was the strength of feeling still felt at the mention of the name of Cromwell.

In addition, the rivalry between Cromwell and King Charles I appears to be never-ending, as pointed out to me by a London cabbie not so long ago. He recounted that in 1950 a group of supporters for Charles I found a lead bust of the monarch in an antique dealer's yard. Having bought it, the group managed to persuade the authorities of St Margaret's Church to erect it on the rear wall of the church, facing Parliament. As a result, Cromwell and Charles I are locked in conflict for eternity. To my mind, this attempted juxtaposition of the two commemorative statues clearly reflects the weakness of Charles I against the long-lasting strength of Oliver Cromwell, as they reside in the very place where our Parliamentary democracy is housed.

Outside of London, closer to his home ground of Cambridgeshire, Cromwell is remembered differently. St Ives has never forgotten him and for all the right reasons. When visiting the town to carry out my research, I took time to admire a statue of him that had been unveiled in October 1901, just two short years after the Westminster statue unveiling. Further investigations revealed a very different ceremony, one that told of the town's enduring pride. At the inaugural church service crowds were led in celebration by massed choirs accompanied by the town band to sing 'O God, Our Help in Ages Past' followed by Psalms 68 and 117, which had been sung by Cromwell and his army after the victory at Dunbar. Imagine the gusto with which they must have sung! The town clearly views Cromwell as their own son, as, in March 2023, more than a hundred years after the statue unveiling, the St Ives Choral Society performed a world premiere of *Cromwell* – an oratorio composed by Tom Randle with libretto by Nick Racklin.

In the opening chapter, I explained how I came to be Lord Naseby and, having taken the title, I decided to see how I could help the public to better understand just how important this unique battle was to the founding of our Parliamentary Democracy. It became my personal crusade.

When I paid my first visit to Naseby, details of the history of the battle were displayed in the parish church with some additional material kept in the library. I soon discovered that there was a group called The Friends of Naseby run by a Mr Martin Marix Evans and I requested a meeting with him to offer my help. He had a desire to create a more permanent exhibition about the battle and to restore the battlefield. But he and the group needed substantial funds to do this. I had discussions with the National Lottery fund who were helpful and, in 2002, they awarded us £70,000. This was to help develop a small museum in the village hall and to fund the restoration of key locations on the battlefield itself. This took the form of a series of viewing platforms from which visitors could be told about the key moments in the battle. I set about engaging local groups and, with the help of Martin Marix Evans, we set up quarterly Saturday visits that included a lecture and guided tour.

Keen to build on this success, Martin and I thought it would be a good idea to have a dedicated museum building for Naseby built on the battlefield itself. We got agreement in principle for a location from a local farmer, and I then prepared a submission for outline planning permission from Daventry District Council, which was approved. The next task was to sound out relevant charities and potential donors. The response was very positive and convinced me that the museum concept was viable.

Sadly, in the middle of this, Martin Marix Evans was taken seriously ill and had to stand down and the new team felt the whole project was too big a risk. I disagreed but nothing was possible without their support. In 2005 I had been made a patron of the Naseby Battlefield Trust but by 2013 all momentum for the project seemed to have gone so I resigned. Today, I still continue to be a member of the Friends of Naseby. I do hope that someone else will take up the cause in the future.

Looking back on the Naseby project, it confirms just what an important part of my life and work Cromwell and his lifelong fight for Parliamentary Democracy has been. From some of my earliest memories of attending the Crusader bible class, to my appointment to the House of Lords as a life peer in recognition for a life in public service, I am grateful for the example that Oliver Cromwell set. Not only in his faith in God but also in his faith in his fellow man and his conviction to fight for fair governance. It feels fitting therefore, knowing that Cromwell was a music lover, to close with a hymn that was written by another Puritan from Bedford, my home of fifty years, who I feel sure Cromwell would have met: John Bunyan (1628–1688):

Who would true valour see,
let him come hither
one here will constant be,
come wind, come weather;
there's no discouragement
shall make him once relent
his first avowed intent
to be a pilgrim

Whoso beset him round
with dismal stories,
do but themselves confound;
his strength the more is.
No lion can him fright;
he'll with a giant fight,
but he will have the right
to be a pilgrim

No goblin nor foul fiend
can daunt his spirit;
he knows he at the end
shall life inherit
Then, fancies fly away;
he'll not fear what men say;
he'll labour night and day
to be a pilgrim

After more than fifty years in Parliament, in both the Commons and the Lords, on every day I have attended Parliament I have passed the statue of Cromwell in front of the House of Commons and have reflected on the huge gift he gave to the world of Parliamentary Democracy. As an American journalist of the nineteenth century said, 'I will go so far as to say that great and powerful as we are, we could find employment for a few Cromwells now' (Townsend, 1884).

I would say we certainly do need people, and particularly leaders, today who will not compromise their principles of having faith in God and in freedom. For living his life by this example, Oliver Cromwell has always been and will continue to be the guiding inspiration for my entire political life.

Appendices

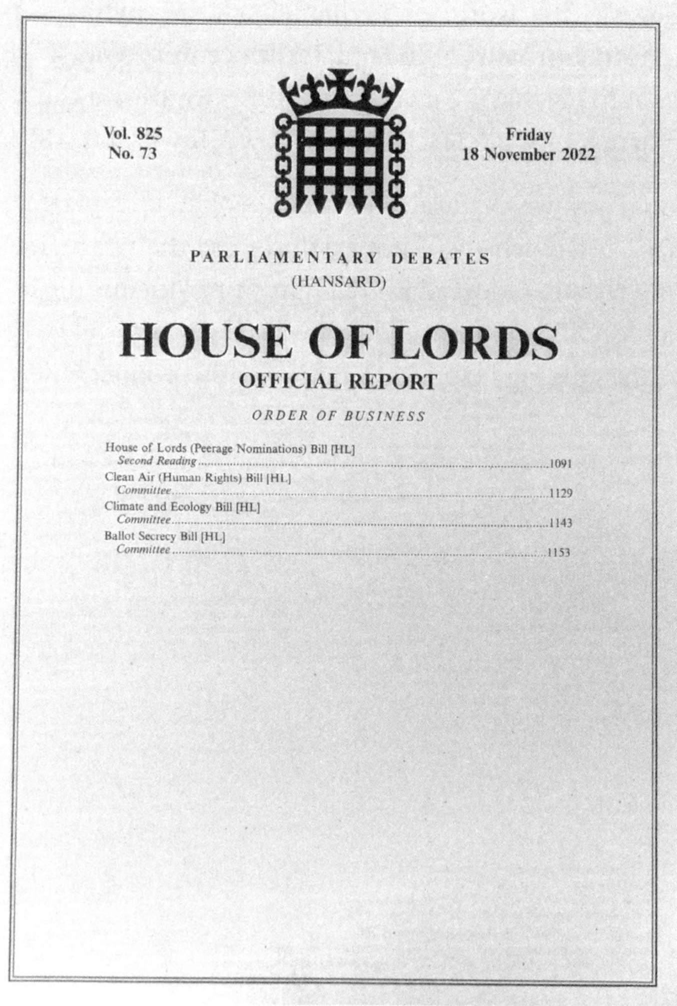

Lord Naseby's Hansard speech re reform [1].

10.53 am

Lord Naseby (Con): My Lords, on Remembrance Sunday last week, I sat in the chapel at Bedford School to pay my respects to the hundreds of young men who gave their lives in two world wars. I was a proud grandfather to see my own granddaughter, as head of the Army CCF joint unit for the two Bedford schools, lay the wreath. It was not long before we sang the familiar hymn, "I Vow to Thee My Country". It is a very moving hymn, and it was a very appropriate one then—and so it is today for Parliament. We are here to give our service and to do our duty to our country. This must not be abused by anyone, in any way.

Being nominated to the House of Lords used to be a recognition of a long and distinguished service—my emphasis is on "long"—in the House of Commons, in industry, commerce and trade unions, or in any walk of life. It is not, and should not be, bestowed lightly or just as a thank you for a couple of years' work for any Prime Minister. It should not be bestowed at the whim of any Prime Minister, however long they may have served.

Returning to that service of dedication, the key words for me are honour, commitment and a spirit of unity. We must remember that we are a revising Chamber, drawing on decades of varying experience across all dimensions of the political make-up. We need men and women with experience of life, who are prepared to question, not afraid to challenge and always seeking to improve legislation. In my judgment, after nearly 50 years in Parliament, there is no place in a modern age for a placement due to birth, as happens with hereditary Peers. Equally, there is no point in having appointees who do not attend or take part; as far as I remember, knighthoods provide that role. I personally welcome all people from all walks of life. I have worked and lived in five countries, and that is where some of my experience has come from.

For me, we must return to the road of reform started in January 2000 when the Royal Commission on the Reform of the House of Lords recommended that the House of Lords Appointments Commission should be established on a statutory basis. I have read again the speeches from that time—I was sitting there then—and I quote briefly the pleas of Viscount Cranborne, who said that

"it is the function of Parliament to be the guardian of our liberties by holding the government continuously to account."

He went on to say that he

"had to watch Parliament weaken progressively, so that it no longer has the strength to command the awe and respect the role demands of it."

He said:

"We complain that the Prime Minister ignores Parliament—and indeed he does. We complain that the press ignore Parliament—and indeed they do. Although we are right to complain, they are right as well. Because of Parliament's weakened position, they can safely ignore us. We no longer have the capacity to inspire enough fear to command their attention."—[*Official Report*, 30/3/1999; cols. 219-20.]

Matters have moved on, with the independent Committee on Standards in Public Life stating that HOLAC—the body we have today—is among the non-statutory regulators in government that

"have a limited or low degree of independence"

which

"falls below what is necessary to ensure effective regulation and maintain public credibility."

The committee concluded:

"Public disquiet on the propriety of appointments to the House of Lords remains a regular feature of our politics".

I believe that this Bill is a very good starting point. It has my wholehearted support and I shall do all I can to ensure that it goes on to the statute book.

10.58 am

Baroness D'Souza (CB): My Lords, as we have heard, incremental changes fare far better than radical reform. Those who believe that the Lords is still mired in the 19th century, if not earlier, now acknowledge evidence of modernisation. We have retirement clauses, standards and monitoring of those standards, and topical Select Committees. On the whole, Peers believe themselves to be working Peers in a 21st-century legislative Chamber, not members of a club. We have the independent Appointments Commission which, in an advisory role, assesses the suitability of prospective Peers and vets the Cross-Benchers.

These incremental changes need protection. They are not set in stone and can be bent to an existing, or future, prevailing political will. The Bill aims to extend and entrench in law the role and function of HOLAC. It simply asks that HOLAC, which does an unenviable job well and with scarce resources, has the right to decree that candidates who come before it must meet the criteria of conspicuous merit and a willingness to work on scrutiny and revision of legislation, and show evidence of probity, more narrowly defined than at present. Decisions would be binding on the Prime Minister of the day.

Undoubtedly, if enacted, the Bill would encroach on the existing unfettered power of the Prime Minister. However, that would in fact occur only very rarely. The commission has let it be known that it is in only a small handful of cases that there has been any question of suitability. However, these few cases are important because they—perhaps disproportionately—provoke much adverse media comment and thus affect the public perception of the House of Lords. A Prime Minister who appoints dubious characters or rides roughshod over HOLAC advice dishonours the House of Lords. A legislative chamber subject to ridicule by the media is easier to dismiss whether by the public or the Government. At present, the Prime Minister can control and undermine the House of Lords simultaneously.

Over the last 20 years and more, the culture within and without Parliament has changed, which argues in favour of a review of the HOLAC terms of reference and working practices. The original vetting criteria are narrow and do not take into account factors such as qualifications, suitability or availability. A review could include redefinition of what constitutes a "working Peer", as well as a formula for addressing the number and balance of Members of the political and Cross-Bench groupings, possibly based on the proportion of votes cast in a general election.

Lord Naseby's Hansard speech re reform [2].

NORTHAMPTONSHIRE CONGREGATIONAL ASSOCIATION.

ANNUAL SPRING MEETINGS.

HONOURING CROMWELL'S MEMORY.

The annual meetings of the Northamptonshire Congregational Association commenced in Northampton on Tuesday. In the morning the members of the Provident Fund met for transaction of business in the Vestry of Doddridge Chapel, and in the evening a well-attended service was held at Commercial-street Church, where the Rev. F. W. Aveling, M.A., B.Sc., at one time pastor of the church, preached a powerful sermon on "The Birth of Oliver Cromwell and Puritan Work for Christ." The devotional service was conducted by the Rev. J. Rippon, of Brigstock; and before the sermon the choir sang the anthem, "Glory to His Name."

Mr. Aveling, who preached for exactly an hour, took as his text the words "Thy Kingdom come. Thy will be done on earth as it is in Heaven" (St. Mathew vi., 10). He said but for Cromwell, toleration on religious matters could not have been obtained. Cromwell cared little about forms of Church government, but very much about real religion. Whatever he did he religiously believed he was doing right in the sight of God. The Puritans learned the grand lesson, and bled for it, that no King, save Jesus Christ, ought to have absolute authority over them. While Charles was plotting secretly against his people, the Constitutional party checked him, stopped him, and won the battle of civil and religious libetry. If Charles had been successful, religious liberty and political freedom must have been crushed. The idea of the Puritan Church was the establishment of Christ's Kingdom upon earth; that the whole of England should become a Church presided over not by sham priests, but by men whose hearts God had consecrated. Had we any higher ideal to-day that that? No. England could only get up enthusiasm for money-making, for sports, for amusements. The modern Londoner went to the theatre, dined at the Hotel Cecil, or rushed after boys selling papers with "all the winners." But some hoped and prayed that London would be found on its knees in prayer once more. Cromwell's foreign policy was not that of the open door, or gracious concessions, or expansion of Empire: his one note of policy was to assist the Protestant world of struggling light against the Papist world of potent darkness. He would have been against the use of the British fleet for the shelling of the Cretans (applause), and with him it would have been impossible that the Armenian massacres should have taken place. (Applause.) They wanted a Puritan revival, a revival of practical religion. They wanted to win men from drink and gambling, to make the homes of the poor better that they might not be tempted to the flaring ginshops; to get the Empire to wash its hands of the sale of opium; to ensure that there should no longer be that great blot upon our national honour by the military system of harlotry in India (applause); that the Prince of Peace should reign, and that war, with its relic of barbarism between civilised nations, should be swept away. (Applause).

A collection in aid of the fund which is being raised for the purposes of Church Extension, was taken.

Honouring Cromwell's memory, 250 years after his death.
Newspaper cutting from the *Mercury*, April 28, 1899.
(Northamptonshire Archives and Heritage Service 216p/CL/65)

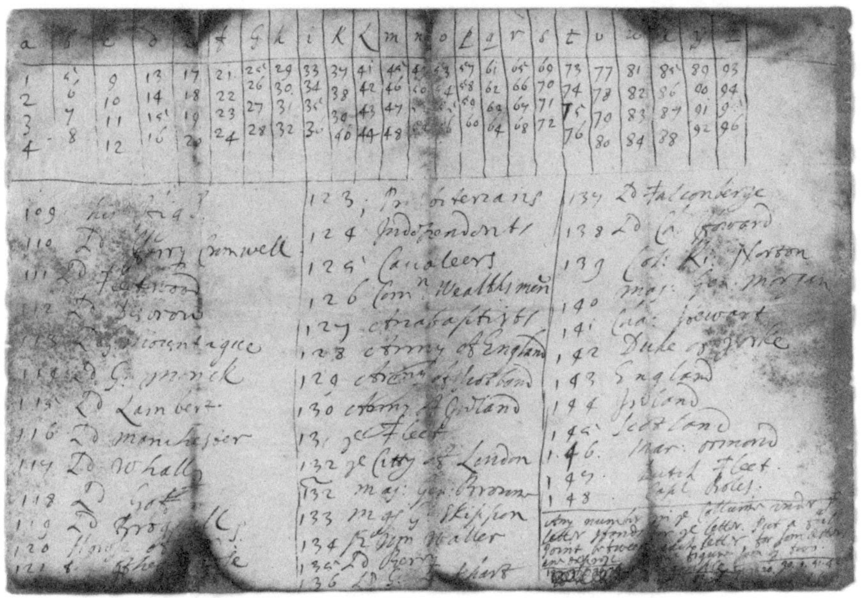

Example of a Civil War cipher, belonging to the Parliamentarian general
Edward Montagu, 2nd Earl of Manchester, who lived at Kimbolton Castle.

48   *Northamptonshire Notes and Queries.*

recited Richard Sitsylt father to David Cecill Grandfather to the said
Sir William Cecill now Lord Burghley; and at this daie William
Sitsylt or Cecill Esquire cozen germane to the said Lord Burghley
removed by one degree only is possessed of the foresaid house of
* Halter ennes in Ewyas land as the heir male of the house of Sitsylt,
and is descended of Philip Cecill elder brother to the said David."

Footnote MS.—"David kept a shop on London Bridg growing
rich bought a Sergeant at " .   .   .   .

Here the MS. is cut through by the binder; one line cannot be
deciphered.

Eccleston, Chester.   J. England Ewen.

414,—Relics of Naseby Fight.—The collection of armour
and other antiquarian objects found on Naseby battle-field, belonging
to captain Ashby Ashby, of Naseby Woolleys, were sold by auction
by Messrs. Holloway, Son, and Price, in February last. Appended
is a list of the most interesting articles; including some portraits
of the Ashby family.

Helmet and 2 horse shoes (£1 2s.)
Old spur, 2 horse shoes, part of antique sword pomel (8s.)
Three horse shoes and cannon ball (14s.)
Three horse shoes, bones, and spear head (11s.)
Curious oval marble vase, an antique bronze mortar, and quantity of
    bullets (£1 4s.)
Rapier, from Naseby Field (£2 15s.)
Part of a stirrup, horse shoe, bones, &c. (10s.)
Bowl of antique British enamelled pottery, said to have been hidden in well
    from soldiers at battle of Naseby, and glass bottle (£2 5s.)
Powder horn, Indian dagger, and three antique slippers (6s.)
Rapier, antique sword and scabbard (£3.)
Engraving "Retreat of a baggage wagon" at the Battle of Naseby, framed
    and glazed (£2 15s.)
Antique iron helmet, cross bow and flint axe (£3 12s 6d.)
Two swords and flint-lock pistol (£2 10s.)
Blunderbuss, axe and club (£1 5s.)
Strong oak table, at which Oliver Cromwell is said to have dined the day before
    the Battle of Naseby (£6.) Bought by Mr. C. H. Davids, Banbury.
Large oil painting "The Lord Keeper Wrighte" (£1 5s.)
Ditto "George Ashby," by Mrs. Verelst (£2.)
Large oil painting "Ashby, of Lowesby," by Coke Smythe (£5.)
Pair Ditto "Prince Henry, son of James I," and "Charles I, when duke of
    York," by Cornelius Janson (£14.)
Cabinet ditto "Countess of Stamford," by Coke Smythe (£1 2s. 6d.)
Large ditto "Quenby Hall (£5.)
Ditto "George Ashby of Quenby" (£6 15s.)
Ditto "George Ashby, The Planter" (£1 10s.)

                                                    J. T.

* Marginal note in MS., " Alterynnis."

Extract from Northamptonshire Notes and Queries,
old series vol III p.48 detailing the Relics of Naseby Fight.
(Northamptonshire Archives and Heritage Service)

Map of Civil War battles.

Oliver Cromwell – Timeline of key dates

25 April 1599	Born in Huntingdon, Cambridgeshire. Fifth of ten children of Robert Cromwell and Elizabeth Steward; the only son to survive to adulthood.
23 April 1616	Enters Sidney Sussex College, Cambridge.
17 April 1617	Death of his father, Robert Cromwell. Oliver leaves Sidney Sussex after completing the first part of the Trivium degree.
22 August 1620	Marries Elizabeth Bourchier, daughter of a prosperous London merchant. They settle in Huntingdon. Nine children follow.
March 1628	Elected MP for Huntingdon.
March 1629	King Charles I dissolves Parliament, beginning the Personal Rule.
1631	Exact date not known – moves to St Ives after disputes with Huntingdon's corporation.
1636	Exact date not known – Moves to Ely to manage family estates; Ely remains his home for life.
April 1640	Elected MP for Cambridge in the Short Parliament.
November 1640	Returned as MP for Cambridge in the Long Parliament.
November 1641	The Grand Remonstrance passed by the Commons.

Autumn 1642	Outbreak of the First Civil War. Cromwell begins active military service.
14 June 1645	Battle of Naseby: decisive victory and first major engagement of the New Model Army.
6 December 1648	Pride's Purge; Cromwell returns to London shortly afterwards.
December 1648	Trial of King Charles I.
30 January 1649	Execution of King Charles I.
20 April 1653	Cromwell dissolves the Rump Parliament.
16 December 1653	Cromwell becomes Lord Protector under the *Instrument of Government*.
3 September 1654	First Protectorate Parliament summoned and meets.
22 January 1655	Cromwell dissolves the First Protectorate Parliament.
17 September 1656	Second Protectorate Parliament meets.
March–May 1657	Cromwell offered the Crown under the *Humble Petition and Advice*.
8 May 1657	Cromwell formally rejects the offer of kingship.
26 June 1657	Cromwell installed for a second term as Lord Protector under the revised constitution.
4 February 1658	Cromwell dissolves the Second Protectorate Parliament.
3 September 1658	Cromwell dies at Whitehall, aged fifty-nine.

Bibliography

With grateful thanks to the staff in the House of Lords Library archives for their help obtain all books, pamphlets and other records.

Akeroyd, A. & Clifford, C. (1999) *Risen from Obscurity: Oliver Cromwell and Huntingdonshire*. Huntingdon: Cromwell Museum.

Bunyan, J. (1659) *The Doctrine of Law and Grace Unfolded*. London.

Bunyan, J. (2003) *The Pilgrim's Progress*. Oxford: Oxford World's Classics.

Cambridge University (c.1600s) *The Rhetoric Syllabus*. Manuscript.

Crawford, L.-G. (1645) 'Intelligence from Northampton', *Perfect Occurrences of Every Day Journal in Parliament*. London.

D'Ewes, S. (1644) *Diary*, entry for 25 November 1644. Manuscript.

Edwards, T. (1646) *Gangraena: or, A Catalogue and Discovery of Many of the Errours, Heresies, Blasphemies and Pernicious Practices of the Sectaries of this Time*. London.

England's New Chains Discovered (1649). London. Leveller pamphlet.

England and Wales. Parliament (1649) *An Act for the Abolishing of the House of Peers*. London.

Firth, C. H. (1910) *The House of Lords during the Civil War*. London: Longmans, Green & Co.

Fitzgibbons, J. (2018) *Cromwell's House of Lords: Politics, Religion and Constitutional Change*. Woodbridge: Boydell Press.

Fraser, A. (1973) *Cromwell: Our Chief of Men*. London: Weidenfeld & Nicolson.

Gaunt, P. (1996) *Oliver Cromwell*. Oxford: Blackwell Publishers.

Head of Zeus / Apollo (2020) *Providence Lost: The Rise and Fall of Cromwell's Protectorate*. London: Head of Zeus.

Holdsworth, R. (c.1630) *Directions for a Student in the Universitie*. Manuscript.

Hutton, R. (2021) *The Making of Oliver Cromwell*. New Haven: Yale University Press.

The Kingdomes Weekly Intelligencer (1645). London. 'Letter from a Gentleman of Northampton'.

Lilburne, J. (1649) *England's New Chains Discovered*. London.

Marix Evans, M. (1998) *Naseby 1645: The Triumph of the New Model Army*. Oxford: Osprey Publishing.

May, T. E. (1989) *Parliamentary Practice*. 21st ed. London: Butterworths.

May, T. E. (2019) *Parliamentary Practice*. 25th ed. London: LexisNexis.

Milton, J. (1654) *Defensio Secunda: The Second Defence of the English People*. London.

Milton, J. (1659) *A Treatise of Civil Power in Ecclesiastical Causes*. London.

Milton, J. (1659) *Considerations Touching the Likeliest Means to Remove Hirelings out of the Church*. London.

Milton, J. (1674) *Paradise Lost*. London.

Moderate Intelligencer (1645). London.

Morrill, J. (ed.) (2022) *The Letters, Writings and Speeches of Oliver Cromwell, Vols. 1–2: 1626–1649*. Oxford: Oxford University Press.

Northamptonshire Record Society (1951) *The Duppa–Isham Correspondence, 1650–1660*, Vol. XVII. Northampton: NRS.

Overton, R. (1646) *A Remonstrance of Many Thousand Citizens, and Other Free-born People of England*. London.

Prynne, W. (1641) *News from Ipswich*. London.

Sharpe, R. (1894) *London and the Kingdom*, Vol. II. London: Longmans, Green & Co.

Sidney Sussex College (1600s) *Statute Book*. Manuscript.

Soldier's Pocket Bible (1643). London.

Townsend, G. A. (1884) *Cromwell and Other Essays*. New York.

Turnbull, M. (2017) *Prince Rupert of the Rhine*. Barnsley: Pen & Sword History.

Wanklyn, M. (2011) *Parliament's Generals: Supreme Command and Politics in the British Wars 1642–1651*. Barnsley: Pen & Sword Military.

Wedgwood, C. V. (1936) *Battlefields in Britain*. London: Jonathan Cape.

Wedgwood, C. V. (1964) *The Trial of Charles I*. London: Macmillan.

Wootton, J. (ed.) (2012) *The Spirit of Dissent: A Commemoration of the Great Ejection 1662*. Winchester: Institute for Theological Partnerships.

Various authors (annual) *Cromwelliana: The Journal of the Cromwell Association*.

Index

READY or Not...
HERE I
COME!

READY or
NOT...
HERE I
CAME!

READY or Not.
HERE I
COME!

READY or
Not...
HERE I
CAME!

READY or Not...
HERE I Came!

READY or Not...

HERE I Come!

READY or NOT...
HERE I COME!

READY or NOT...
HERE I CAME!

READY or Not...
HERE I Come!

READY or
Not...
HERE I
Came!

READY or NOT...
HERE I Come!

READY or Not...
HERE I
COME!
x

READY or
NOT...
HERE I
CAME!

READY or
Not...
HERE I
CAME!

READY or
NOT...
HERE I
COME!

READY or NOT...
HERE I COME!

READY or Not...
HERE I
Came!

READY or Not...
HERE I
CAME!

READY or NOT...
HERE I COME!

READY or
NOT...
HERE I
Came!

READY or NOT...
HERE I CAME!

READY or NOT...
HERE I
COME!

READY or NOT...
HERE I COME!

READY or NOT...
NOT.
HERE I
COME!

READY or Not...
HERE I
Came!

READY or NOT...
HERE I CAME!

READY or NOT...
HERE I COME!

READY or NOT...
HERE I COME!

READY or Not...
HERE I Came!

READY or Not...
HERE I CAME!

READY or NOT...
HERE I COME!

READY or NOT...
HERE I COME!

READY or Not...
HERE I
COME!

READY or NOT...
HERE I
CAME!

READY or NOT...
HERE I COME!

READY or NOT...
HERE I CAME!

READY or
NoT...
HERE I
Came!

READY or
NOT...
HERE I
CAME!

READY or NOT...
HERE I COME!

READY or NOT...
HERE I COME!

READY or Not...
HERE I
Came!

READY or NOT...
HERE I CAME!

READY or NOT...
HERE I COME!

READY or NOT...
HERE I CAME!

READY or NOT...
HERE I COME!

READY or
NOT...
HERE I
CAME!

READY or Not...
HERE I Came!

READY or NOT...
HERE I COME!

READY or NOT...
NOT...
HERE I
Come!

READY or
Not...
HERE I
Come!

READY or
Not...
HERE I
COME!

READY or Not...
HERE I COME!

READY or Not...
HERE I Came!

READY or
Not...
HERE I
Came!

READY or NOT...
HERE I COME!

READY or NOT...
HERE I COME!

READY or NOT...
HERE I COME!

READY or Not...
HERE I Came!

READY or Not...
HERE I COME!

READY or NOT...
HERE I COME!

READY or Not...
HERE I CaMe!

READY or Not...
HERE I Came!

READY or NOT...
HERE I COME!

READY or NOT...
HERE I CAME!

READY or NOT...
HERE I
CaME!

READY or
NOT...
HERE I
COME!

READY or NOT...
HERE I COME!

READY or NOT...
HERE I CAME!

READY or NOT...
HERE I COME!

READY or NOT...
HERE I COME!

READY or
NOT...
HERE I
COME!

READY or
NOT...
HERE I
COME!

READY or NOT...
HERE I CAME!

READY or Not...
HERE I
Came!

READY or
NOT...
HERE I
COME!

READY or Not...
HERE I
Came!

READY or NOT...
HERE I
COME!

READY or Not...
HERE I Came!

READY or NOT...
HERE I CAME!

READY or Not...
HERE I Came!

READY or NOT...
HERE I CAME!

READY or
NOT...
HERE I
CaMe!

READY or NOT...
HERE I COME!

READY or NoT...
HERE I CAME!

READY or
NoT...
HERE I
CAME!

READY or NOT...
HERE I CAME!

READY or NOT...
HERE I COME!

READY or
NOT...
HERE I
COME!

READY or
Not...
HERE I
Came!

READY or NOT...
HERE I CAME!

READY or NOT...
HERE I COME!

READY or NOT...
HERE I CAME!

READY or Not...
HERE I Came!

READY or
NOT...
HERE I
COME!

READY or
Not...
HERE I
Come!

READY or NOT...
HERE I Came!

READY or
NOT...
HERE I
Come!

READY or Not..
HERE I
CaMe!

READY or NOT...
HERE I COME!

READY or Not...
HERE I Came!

READY or Not...
HERE I Came!

READY or Not...
HERE I Come!

READY or NOT...
HERE I CAME!

READY or NOT...
HERE I COME!

READY or Not...
HERE I
Come!

READY or Not...
HERE I Come!

READY or NoT...
HERE I COMe!

READY or NoT...
HERE I
CaMe!

READY or NOT...
HERE I COME!

READY or
NOT...
HERE I
COME!

READY or
NOT...
HERE I
COME!

READY or NOT...
HERE I COME!

READY or NOT...
HERE I CAME!

READY or NOT...
HERE I
Come!

READY or NOT...
HERE I Come!

READY or Not...

HERE I Came!

READY or Not...
HERE I Came!

READY or Not...
HERE I Come!

READY or NOT...
HERE I COME!